W9-BAG-238

DISCARD

Mastercam®

Version 8 Mill/Design
Applications Guide

Mastercam Version 8
© 1984 - 2000 CNC Software, Inc.

Mastercam® Version 8 Applications Guide - Design and Mill

Date: February 15, 2000
Copyright © 1984 - 2000 CNC Software, Inc. - All rights reserved.
First Printing: February 15, 2000
Software: Mastercam Mill Version 8
ISBN: 1-883310-17-2

Notice

CNC Software, Inc. reserves the right to make improvements to the CAD/CAM system described in this manual at any time and without notice.

Software License

You have the non-exclusive right to use the enclosed program. This program may only be used on a single computer. You may physically transfer the program from one computer to another provided that the program is used on only one computer at a time. You may not electronically transfer the program from one computer to another over a network. You may not distribute copies of the program or documentation to others. You may not modify or translate the program or related documentation without the prior written consent of CNC Software, Inc.

Disclaimer Of All Warranties And Liability

CNC Software, Inc. makes no warranties, either express or implied, with respect to this manual or with respect to the software described in this manual, its quality, performance, merchantability, or fitness for any particular purpose. CNC Software, Inc. software is sold or licensed "as is." The entire risk as to its quality and performance is with the buyer. Should the CAD/CAM system prove defective following its purchase, the buyer (and not CNC Software, Inc., its distributor, or its retailer) assumes the entire cost of all necessary servicing, repair, of correction and any incidental or consequential damages. In no event will CNC Software, Inc. be liable for direct, indirect, or consequential damages resulting from any defect in the software, even if CNC Software, Inc. has been advised of the possibility of such damages. Some jurisdictions do not allow the exclusion or limitation of implied warranties or liability for incidental or consequential damages, so the above limitation or exclusion may not apply to you.

Copyrights

This manual is copyrighted. All rights are reserved. This document may not, in whole or part, be copied, photocopied, reproduced, translated or reduced to any electronic medium or machine readable form without prior consent, in writing, from CNC Software, Inc.

Trademarks

Mastercam is a registered trademark of CNC Software, Inc.
Microsoft, the Microsoft logo, MS, and MS-DOS are registered trademarks of Microsoft Corporation; Windows, Windows 95, and Windows NT are registered trademarks of Microsoft Corporation. Mastercam Verify is created in conjunction with Sirius Systems Corporation.

Printed in the United States of America.

This book was printed on recycled paper.

Table of Contents

1 Getting Started with Mastercam

About Using and Learning Mastercam

Welcome to Mastercam Version 8. Mastercam is a powerful CAD/CAM application that lets you design parts and choose from 2- through 5-axis milling, turning, wire EDM, lasers, mold base development, surface, and solid modeling.

To help you learn Mastercam, extensive online help and this Applications Guide accompany the product.

About This Applications Guide

This guide teaches you the practical and efficient use of Mastercam Design and Mill software. It is a self-training aid for both the beginning and experienced Mastercam user.

To get you started, the guide provides a short tutorial on learning the product user interface and then launches into many practical projects for you to complete. The projects are designed to show you efficient ways to design and mill a real-world part.

Note: To complete most of the projects in this guide, you must install Level 1 of Mastercam Mill Version 8 on your PC. To complete all of the projects in this guide, you must install Level 3 of Mastercam Mill Version 8 on your PC. Refer to the installation instructions that accompany your product.

How This Guide is Organized

This guide is organized into a series of exercises that progress from the basics of designing a 2D part and creating a contour toolpath to more complicated subjects such as advanced pocket toolpaths and surface machining. The guide also shows you how to use the Operations Manager to edit, regenerate, and create the output code that is used by a CNC machine.

This guide also introduces you to the powerful feature called Associativity that links geometry with toolpath, tool, and material information and creates a complete operation. If any part of the associative operation changes, the other related pieces can be regenerated without having to recreate the whole operation.

The guide is organized into the following chapters:

1	**Getting Started with Mastercam**	Includes conventions, online help, technical support information, and a tutorial on learning the Mastercam user interface.
2	**Creating a 2D Part and Contour Toolpath**	Contains 2D design and contour toolpath creation.
3	**Modifying a 2D Contour Toolpath**	Describes how to make changes to a 2D contour toolpath.
4	**Rotating 2D Geometry and Contour Toolpath**	Shows how to use the Transform, Rotate function to create a 2D part and a contour toolpath. Includes rotating a toolpath and geometry.
5	**Making a 3D Wireframe Design and 3D Contour Toolpath**	Describes how to create a 3D wireframe part and a contour toolpath for the part.
6	**Creating Drill Toolpaths**	Includes several types of drill toolpaths, including programming a drill toolpath at multiple Z depths.
7	**Creating Facing and Pocket Toolpaths**	Illustrates the basic concepts involved in creating pocket toolpaths. Includes different cutting methods, chaining, facing, and entry points.
8	**Using Advanced Pocket and Contour Toolpaths**	Covers more advanced methods of creating pocket and contour toolpaths. Includes remachining, depth cuts, tapered walls, and island facing. Also introduces the Toolpath Editor.
9	**Importing, Grouping, and Saving Operations**	Shows how to create drill and pocket toolpaths, and how to use the Import/Save functions to apply these operations to similar parts. Shows how to create operational groups.

10	**Creating Circle Toolpaths**	Shows how to create circle mill, thread mill, and automatic arc drill toolpaths.
11	**Creating and Machining Surfaces**	Describes how to create ruled, loft, and coons surfaces and some surface toolpaths. Includes information about what types of surfaces to create for different wireframe geometry.
12	**Choosing a Surface Type**	Focuses on the different surfaces you can create with Mastercam and shows examples of each surface type.
13	**Surface Roughing**	Describes some of the roughing toolpaths you can use in surface machining.
14	**Surface Finishing**	Shows some of the finishing toolpaths you can use in surface machining. Includes finish parallel steep, radial, project, flowline, contour, shallow, and scallop toolpaths.
15	**Creating a Multiaxis Toolpath**	Shows how to create curve and swarf 5-axis toolpaths on parts with surfaces.
	Appendix - Drawings	Contains dimensioned drawings of all the parts used in this guide.
	Glossary	Comprehensive list of Mastercam terms.
	Mastercam Shortcut Keys	Shows a list of keyboard shortcuts.

About the Sample Parts Used in the Exercises

The sample parts for all the exercises in this guide are located in the Mcam8\Common\Tutorials directory. Before you begin working with the sample parts, create a separate folder to save them in.

> IMPORTANT: Using the saved part ensures that the original sample part does not get modified and that you can go back to the original part if you need to start over.

Who Should Use This Guide

This guide is designed for Mastercam users of all skill levels.

Before starting, you should have basic knowledge of the CAD/CAM process and of Microsoft® Windows®. Refer to your Windows documentation for more information.

Typographic Conventions Used

This guide uses several typographic conventions:

Bold type identifies any portion of the Mastercam interface that you select, including menu options, dialog box options, and buttons. (Example: the **MAIN MENU**)

Brackets [ ] identify keys that you press on the keyboard, such as [Enter], [Esc], etc.

Italic text identifies messages that display in the prompt area of the Mastercam main screen where you enter values. (Example: *Enter coordinates*)

Note: A point of information related to the preceding text.

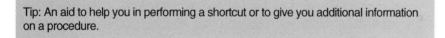

Tip: An aid to help you in performing a shortcut or to give you additional information on a procedure.

The [Esc] key is normally used throughout Mastercam to back up to the previous level of the menu structure. When the keyboard convention does not apply, the use of the [Esc] key is explained in the text.

As shown below, check boxes adjacent to buttons on a dialog box activate or deactivate the button. If the check box is selected, the button is active and can be chosen to edit the related options. If the check box is not selected, the button cannot be chosen and all features associated with the button are disabled.

Help Beyond This Guide

Online Help

Online help contains the latest and most up-to-date information about Mastercam. Use online help as a tool for using Mastercam. To access online help, press a Help button on a dialog box or press [Alt+H] at any menu while you are working in Mastercam.

Dealers

If you have a question about Mastercam and have not been able to locate the answer in this guide or the online help, contact your local Mastercam dealer. Mastercam is sold and distributed through a network of dealers.

Technical Support

If you do not remember who your dealer is or if your dealer is unavailable, you can call CNC Software Support Services Monday through Friday, 8:00 a.m. - 6:00 p.m., USA Eastern Standard Time.

When calling CNC Software, Inc. for technical support, please follow these guidelines:

◆ Be sure you have already tried to contact your Mastercam dealer regarding the problem or question. Your chances of getting complete support are much better if you do.

◆ Be ready to describe the problem in detail. Write down what happened, particularly if you cannot call immediately after the problem occurs.

◆ Be in front of your computer when you call.

◆ If possible, try to duplicate the problem before calling. Our Support Services technician may require you to duplicate the problem while you are on the phone.

◆ When you call, have ready a complete description of your hardware, including your operating system (OS), central processing unit (CPU), mouse, and memory.

You can also leave a message for CNC Support Services twenty-four hours a day, seven days a week via our e-mail or web site addresses or the BBS. A member of our technical support staff will return your e-mail or call you on the next business day. Keep the following information on hand in case you need to reach us:

Important Information	
Address	CNC Software, Inc. 671 Old Post Road Tolland, Connecticut, 06084-9970 USA
Phone	(860) 875-5006
Fax	(860) 872-1565
BBS	(860) 871-8050
TELNET and ftp://	206.231.172.100
Internet Address	http://www.mastercam.com
E-mail	support@mastercam.com

Additional Resources

◆ For information on training, contact your Mastercam dealer.

◆ *FASTech Multimedia Training* (*FMMT*). For additional information about this multimedia training product, call FASTech, Inc.: (419) 425-2233, in the USA.

Exercise 1 – Learning the Mastercam Interface

This exercise shows you how to navigate through Mastercam. You will:
- ◆ **Launch the application**
- ◆ **Make selections from the menus and toolbar**
- ◆ **Use program prompts for guidance**
- ◆ **Design a simple part that you'll use in a later exercise**

▶ *Launch Mastercam*

You must have Level 1 of Mastercam Mill Version 8 installed on your PC to complete most of the milling exercises in this guide (and Level 3 is required for the last few chapters).

1. Choose
   - ◆ **Windows Start menu**
   - ◆ **Programs, Mastercam, Mill 8**

Note: If you cannot open Mastercam, refer to your installation instructions included in a separate document.

2. The main Mastercam window appears, as shown below.

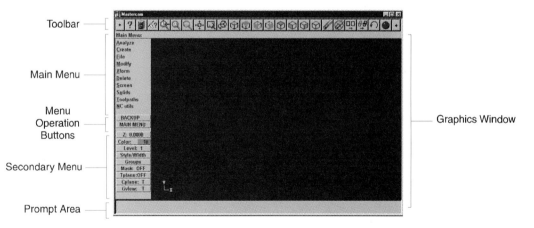

Toolbar

Main Menu

Menu
Operation
Buttons

Secondary Menu

Prompt Area

Graphics Window

▶ *Use the Main Menu*

The Main Menu contains the primary functions you use in Mastercam.

1. Choose
   - ◆ **MAIN MENU**
   - ◆ **Create**
   - ◆ **Point**
   - ◆ **Position**

2. Notice that the prompt area at the bottom left of the screen displays the message *Create point: specify a point.*

▶ *Use the prompt area*

The prompt area displays a message to help you understand what action to take. It is also the screen location where you enter values.

1. Without moving your mouse, type **0,0**.

2. Notice that the values you type (the coordinates) appear in the prompt area as you type.

Enter coordinates: 0,0

3. Press [Enter] to display the point at position 0,0.

4. Press [F9] to display the construction origin. The graphics window should look like the following picture.

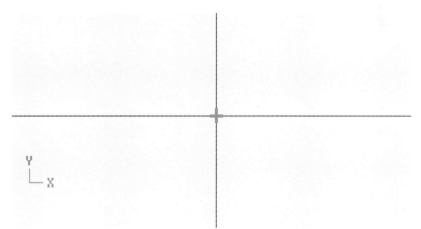

Exercise 2 – Designing a rectangle

This exercise shows you how to design a simple rectangle with fillets. You will:

- ◆ **Use the Create, Rectangle function**
- ◆ **Use the Create, Fillet function**
- ◆ **Save the part for use in an exercise in Chapter 9.**

▶ *Create a rectangle*

In this task, you will create a rectangle with the center at 0,0.

1. Choose
   - ◆ **MAIN MENU**
   - ◆ **Create**
   - ◆ **Rectangle**
   - ◆ **1 Point**

2. Enter the values shown on the dialog.

3. Choose **OK**.

4. Drag the cross-hairs cursor near to the point you created earlier until you see a small white square appear over the point.

5. Click the mouse button to position the rectangle so that its center is at the coordinates 0,0. Notice that the rectangle function is still active (in case you want to create another rectangle).

6. Press [Esc] to exit the rectangle function.

Note: If you accidentally create more than one rectangle, you can delete the unwanted geometry by choosing MAIN MENU, Delete and selecting the lines to delete.

Your part should look like the following picture.

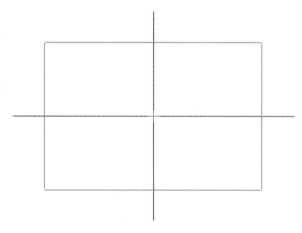

▶ *Create corner fillets*

A fillet is an arc tangent to two entities. Create fillets to make rounded corners on the rectangle with a 3/8 inch radius.

1. Choose
    - ◆ **MAIN MENU**
    - ◆ **Create**
    - ◆ **Fillet**
    - ◆ **Radius**

2. *Enter the fillet radius* in the prompt area: **0.375** and press [Enter].

3. Select the lines at positions 1 and 2.

4. Repeat Step 3 to create fillets at the other three corners.

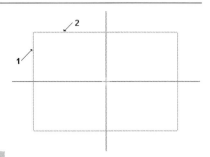

Tip: When you move the cursor close to an entity during selection, it turns white.

Your part should look like the following picture.

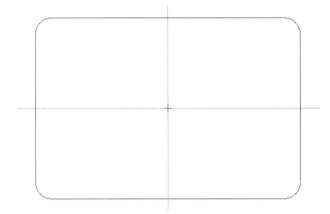

▶ *Save the file*

1. If you have not already done so, create a folder, such as "Applications Guide Exercises" to save your files.

2. Choose
   - ◆ **MAIN MENU**
   - ◆ **File**
   - ◆ **Save**

3. Save the file as **cover.mc8** in the folder you created for your files. You will use this file in Chapter 9.

Note: It is a good idea to save your file frequently as you work. This way, if you make an error, you can choose File, Get to open a previously saved version of the file. Each time you successfully finish one exercise, save your file. You can press [Alt + A] to use the AutoSave feature.

2 *Creating a 2D Part and Contour Toolpath*

This chapter guides you through the design of a 2D part and the creation of a contour toolpath for the part. After you create the toolpath, you make changes to the part and update the toolpath accordingly.

Exercise 1 – Designing the Part

This exercise shows you how to use several basic drawing functions to create the elbow part shown in the picture below. You will:

◆ **Create points, lines, arcs, and fillets**
◆ **Mirror and rotate lines**
◆ **Trim unnecessary lines and arcs**

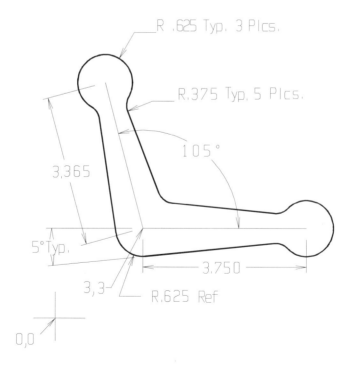

▶ *Create a point*

Create a point of origin to center the drawing on the screen.

1. Choose
   - ◆ **File, New**
   - ◆ **MAIN MENU**
   - ◆ **Create**
   - ◆ **Point**
   - ◆ **Position**

2. *Enter coordinates.* **3,3**

> Tip: When you begin typing the "3," it displays in the prompt area (lower left). Press [ENTER] when done.

3. Choose the **Fit** button on the toolbar to center the point in the graphics window.

▶ *Create the construction lines*

Draw lines to help construct the other entities.

1. Choose
   - ◆ **MAIN MENU**
   - ◆ **Create**
   - ◆ **Line**
   - ◆ **Polar**

2. Select the point.

3. *Enter the angle in degrees.* **0**

> Tip: Pass the cursor over the point. When an open square displays, click the mouse button.

4. *Enter the line length.* **3.75**

5. Select the same point.

> Tip: Press [Enter] after entering the value(s) in the prompt area.

6. *Enter the angle in degrees.* **105**

7. *Enter the line length.* **3.365**

8. Press [F9] to display the construction origin. The part should look like the following picture, with lines originating at position 3,3.

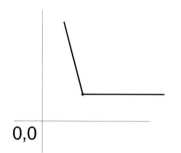

Note: You must press [F9] again to get rid of the axis lines.

▶ *Create an arc*

You use arcs to create the curved ends and outside bend of the part.

1. Choose
   - ◆ **MAIN MENU**
   - ◆ **Create**
   - ◆ **Arc**
   - ◆ **Polar**
   - ◆ **Sketch**

2. Select the line endpoint at position 1, as shown in the picture to the right.

3. *Enter the radius.* **.625**

4. Select at position 2 then at position 3.

Note: When you select a position that does not lie on a point, you are selecting an approximate location.

5. Select the origin point at position 4.

6. *Enter the radius.* **.625**

7. Select at position 5 then at position 6.

8. Select the line endpoint at position 7.

9. *Enter the radius.* **.625**

10. Select at position 8 then at position 9. The part should look like the picture shown on the right.

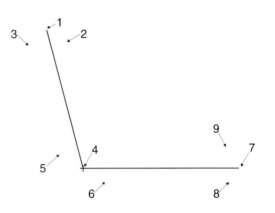

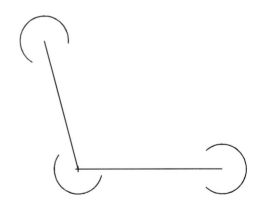

▶ *Rotate the lines*

Rotate the lines as a first step in creating the outside lines.

1. Choose
   - ◆ **MAIN MENU**
   - ◆ **Xform**
   - ◆ **Rotate**

2. Select the line at position 1.

3. Choose **Done**.

4. Select the line endpoint at position 2.

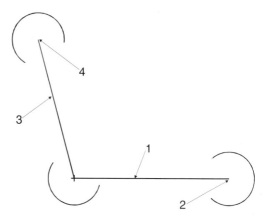

5. Enter the values shown on the following dialog box.

Tip: Refer to the drawing on page 2-1 to see the location of the 5° angle, (between position 3 and 1 as shown above).

6. Choose **OK**.

Note: The system identifies the original lines (Group) and rotated lines (Result) with different colors.

7. Select the line at position 3.

8. Choose **Done**.

9. Select the line endpoint at position 4.

10. Enter the values shown on the following dialog box.

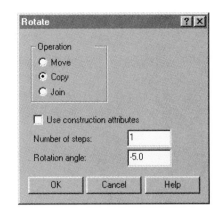

11. Choose **OK**.

 12. Choose the **Screen-Clear colors** button on the toolbar to return the lines to their original color. The part should look like the following picture.

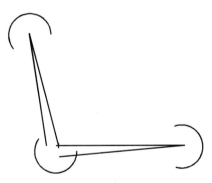

 Create parallel lines tangent to the arcs

Move the 5° angled lines to their correct position, tangent to the curved ends.

1. Choose
   - ◆ **MAIN MENU**
   - ◆ **Create**
   - ◆ **Line**
   - ◆ **Parallel**
   - ◆ **Arc**

2. Select the line at position 1.

3. Select the arc at position 2.

Note: This function creates 2 lines. You must pick the line you want to keep.

4. Select the bottom line to keep.

5. Select the line at position 3.

6. Select the arc at position 4.

7. Select the left line to keep.

8. Choose
   - ◆ **MAIN MENU**
   - ◆ **Delete**

9. Delete the lines at positions 1 and 2.

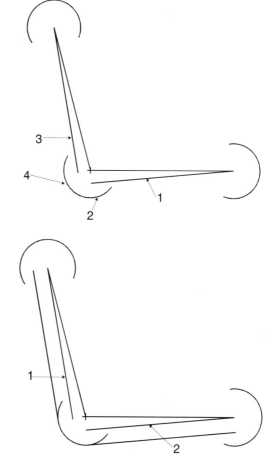

 Mirror the lines about the construction lines

Create the inside lines of the elbow by mirroring the outside lines.

1. Choose
   - ◆ **MAIN MENU**
   - ◆ **Xform**
   - ◆ **Mirror**

2. Select the line at position 1.

3. Choose **Done**.

4. Select the line to mirror about at position 2.

5. Choose
   - ◆ **Copy**
   - ◆ **OK**

6. Select the line at position 3.

7. Choose **Done**.

8. Select the line to mirror about at position 4.

9. Choose
   - ◆ **Copy**
   - ◆ **OK**

10. Clear the screen colors. Your part should look like the picture shown at right.

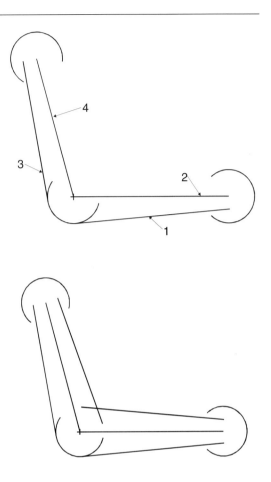

▶ *Create the 3/8 inch fillets*

Create fillets to join the outside lines to the arcs. Also create a fillet at the inside bend of the elbow.

Note: This function also trims the lines to the fillets.

1. Choose
   - ◆ **MAIN MENU**
   - ◆ **Create**
   - ◆ **Fillet**
   - ◆ **Radius**

2. *Enter the fillet radius.* **.375**

3. Select the line at position 1.

4. Select the arc at position 2. Your part should look like the following picture.

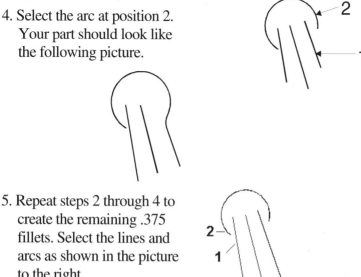

5. Repeat steps 2 through 4 to create the remaining .375 fillets. Select the lines and arcs as shown in the picture to the right.

> Tip: Select the two crossing lines to create the fillet inside the elbow bend. If you make a mistake while filleting, choose the Undo button or press [Alt + U].

The part with the completed fillets should look like the picture below.

▶ *Trim the arcs to the lines*

1. Choose
   - ◆ **MAIN MENU**
   - ◆ **Modify**
   - ◆ **Trim**
   - ◆ **3 entities**

2. Select the line at position 1.

3. Select the line at position 2.

4. Select the arc at position 3.

5. Delete the construction lines at positions 4 and 5.

6. Delete the point at position 6. Your finished part should look like the following picture.

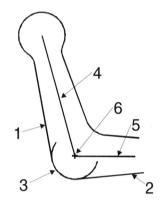

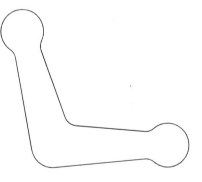

▶ *Save the file*

1. Choose
   - ◆ **MAIN MENU**
   - ◆ **File**
   - ◆ **Save**

2. Save the file as **elbow.mc8** in the folder you created for your files.

Exercise 2 – Creating the Contour Toolpath

This exercise shows you the basic steps for creating a contour toolpath. A toolpath shows how material is removed along a cutter path. A contour toolpath removes material along a cutter path defined by a curve or chain of curves.

The toolpath you will create is for the part you created in Exercise 1. The finished toolpath should look like the picture below. You will use:
- ◆ **Toolpaths, Contour**
- ◆ **Chaining**
- ◆ **Tool and contour parameters**
- ◆ **Backplot and post processing**

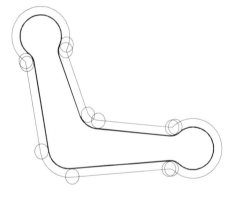

▶ *Choose the toolpath type and chain the toolpath*

Chaining is the selection of one or more sets of curves (lines, arcs and/or splines) in which the curves have adjoining endpoints (points can also be chained).

1. Open **elbow.mc8**.

2. Choose
- ◆ **MAIN MENU**
- ◆ **Toolpaths**
- ◆ **Contour**

3. Save the NCI file as **elbow.nci**

Note: The NCI file is an intermediate NC file Mastercam uses. The system automatically creates the .nci file extension.

4. Select at position 1 to start the chain.

Note: Make sure you select the line and not the endpoint of the arc. An arrow displays showing the chaining direction. Make sure the chaining direction is clockwise, as indicated by the arrowhead.

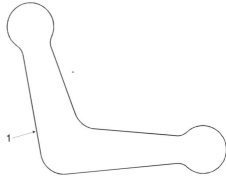

The entire part should highlight. If it does not, there may be a gap between two entities.

5. Choose **Done.**

▶ ### *Select a tool from the library*

Each toolpath is associated with the tool that will machine the part.

1. Right-click in the tool display area. A right-click menu displays as shown in the following picture.

```
Tool parameters | Contour parameters |
        Left 'click' on tool to select; right 'click' to edit or define new tool

                    Get tool from library...
                    Create new tool...
                    Get operations from library...
                    Job setup...

   Tool #    1        Tool name            Tool dia   0.5      Corner radius  0.0

   Head #    -1       Feed rate   6.4176   Program #  0        Spindle speed  1069

   Dia. offset  41    Plunge rate 6.4176   Seq. start  100     Coolant        Off

   Len. offset  1     Retract rate 6.4176  Seq. inc.   2

                                                                      Change NCI...
   Comment
                                     ☑ Home pos...   ☐ Ref point...  ☑ Misc. values...
                                     ☐ Rotary axis... ☑ T/C plane... ☑ Tool display...
   ☐ To batch                                                        ☐ Canned text...

                                               OK        Cancel       Help
```

2. Choose **Get tool from library**.

3. Select the ½" flat endmill as shown on the following dialog box.

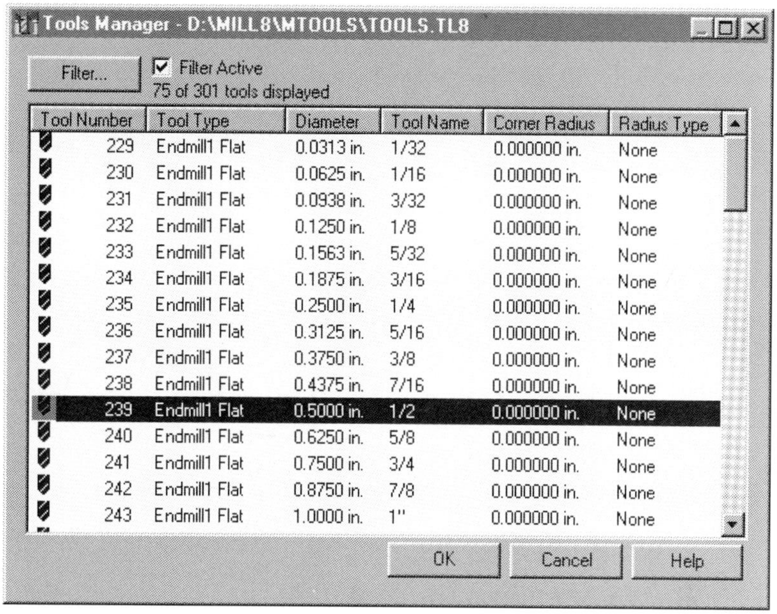

4. Choose **OK**. The tool appears in the tool display area as shown in the following picture.

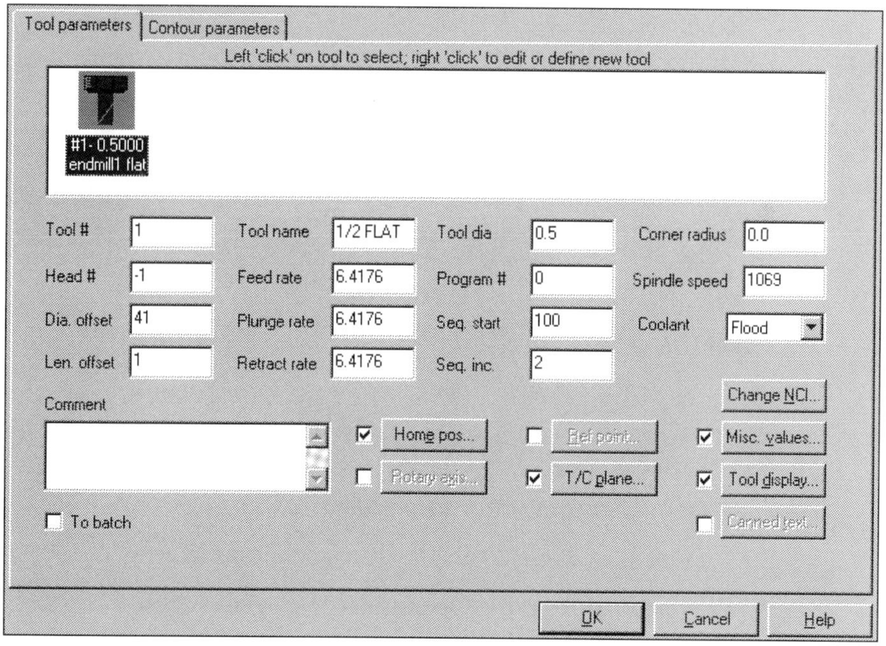

Note: You can enter the values you want in this dialog box or you can choose OK to accept the default values.

5. Choose **OK** to accept the default values. The toolpath should look like the following picture.

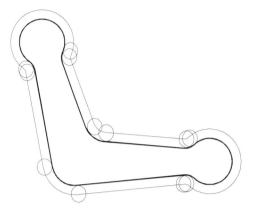

Note: The circles represent the movement of the tool and lines of NC code.

▶ *Backplot to view the toolpath*

Backplotting displays the path the tool takes to cut the part and lets you catch errors in the program before you machine the part.

1. Choose **Operations** to open the Operations Manager.

2. Choose **Backplot** from the Operations Manager.

3. Choose **Step** from the Backplot menu.

4. Use the mouse to choose **Step** from the Backplot menu or press [S] repeatedly to step through the toolpath you created.

> Tip: You can press and hold both mouse buttons on the word Step to quickly run through the steps.

5. When the backplot is complete, choose **OK**.

▶ *Post the operation*

Note: In this procedure, you use the system default post processor. For more information on the types of post processors available in Mastercam, refer to the Mastercam Post Processor User Guide. To obtain a copy of this manual, contact your Mastercam dealer.

1. Choose **BACKUP** to display the Operations Manager.

2. Choose **Post** from the Operations Manager.

3. Enter the values shown on the following dialog box.

Post processing
Active post
Change Post
C:\MCAM8\MILL\POSTS\MPFAN.PST
NCI file
Save NCI file
Edit
Overwrite
Ask
NC file
Save NC file
Edit
Overwrite
NC extension
Ask
.nc
Send
Send to machine
Comm...
OK
Cancel
Help

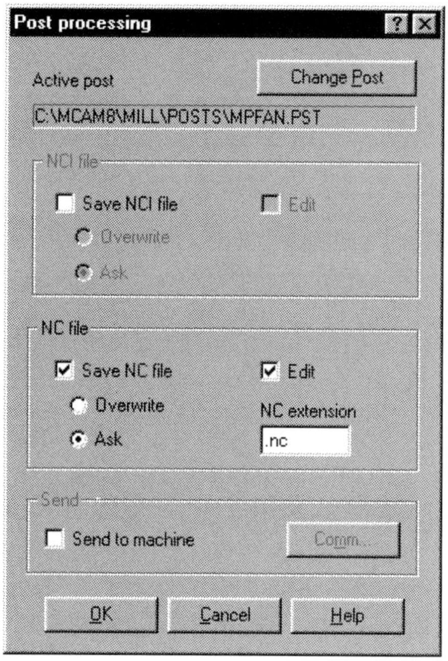

4. Choose **OK**.
5. Save the NC file as **elbow.nc**. The NC code displays as shown in the following picture.

Note: The system automatically creates the .nc file extension.

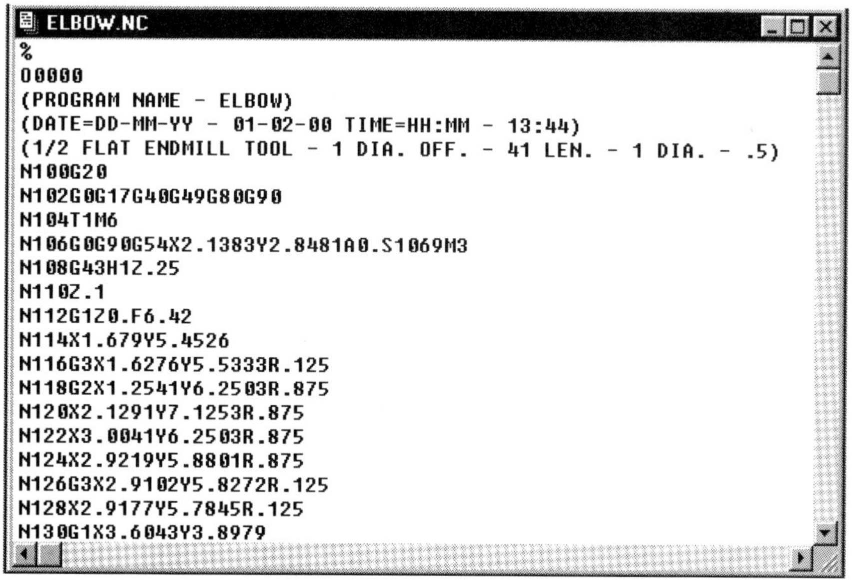

ELBOW.NC
%
O0000
(PROGRAM NAME - ELBOW)
(DATE=DD-MM-YY - 01-02-00 TIME=HH:MM - 13:44)
(1/2 FLAT ENDMILL TOOL - 1 DIA. OFF. - 41 LEN. - 1 DIA. - .5)
N100G20
N102G0G17G40G49G80G90
N104T1M6
N106G0G90G54X2.1383Y2.8481A0.S1069M3
N108G43H1Z.25
N110Z.1
N112G1Z0.F6.42
N114X1.679Y5.4526
N116G3X1.6276Y5.5333R.125
N118G2X1.2541Y6.2503R.875
N120X2.1291Y7.1253R.875
N122X3.0041Y6.2503R.875
N124X2.9219Y5.8801R.875
N126G3X2.9102Y5.8272R.125
N128X2.9177Y5.7845R.125
N130G1X3.6043Y3.8979

Note: The code displayed in the window is the output code used by the NC machine. It is saved as an NC file and is not contained in the MC8 file. However, an intermediate file with an NCI extension is generated each time you create a toolpath and can be used to post process and create NC files.

6. Close the NC code window.

7. Save the file as **elbow.mc8**.

Exercise 3 – Making Changes to the Toolpath

This exercise shows you how to easily make changes to a toolpath with Mastercam. For this part, you need to change how the tool enters the material. Plunging directly into the part is not desirable because of the dwell marks left behind at the tool entry spot. In this exercise, you add entry and exit passes to the toolpath to eliminate the dwell marks. The finished toolpath should look like the following picture. The functions you will use are:

- ◆ **Operations Manager**
- ◆ **Contour parameters**
- ◆ **Lead in/out**
- ◆ **Regenerate the toolpath**

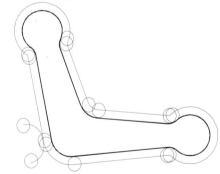

▶ *Open the file and access the toolpath parameters*

1. Open **elbow.mc8**.

2. Press [Alt+O] to open the Operations Manager.

3. Choose the **Parameters** icon.

4. Choose the **Contour parameters** tab.

```
⊟ Ꮐ Toolpath Group #1
   ⊟ 🔩 1 - Contour
         📄 Parameters
         🔩 #1 - 0.5000 ENDMILL1 FLAT - 1/2
         ⊞ Geometry - (1) chain(s)
         ▤ D:\MILL8\NCI\ELBOW.NCI - 3.9K
```

5. Select the **Lead in/out** check box and choose the **Lead in/out** button.

6. Enter the values shown on the following dialog box.

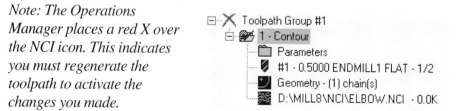

Note: The line length and arc radius may be entered as a percentage of the tool diameter, or as a distance.

7. Choose **OK** twice.

Note: The Operations Manager places a red X over the NCI icon. This indicates you must regenerate the toolpath to activate the changes you made.

```
⊟ ✗ Toolpath Group #1
   ⊟ 🔩 1 - Contour
         📄 Parameters
         🔩 #1 - 0.5000 ENDMILL1 FLAT - 1/2
         ⊞ Geometry - (1) chain(s)
         ▤ D:\MILL8\NCI\ELBOW.NCI - 0.0K
```

8. Choose **Regen Path**. The updated toolpath should look like the following picture.

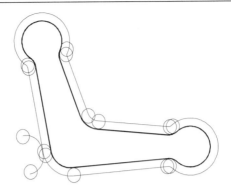

9. Choose **OK**.

10. Save the file as **elbow.mc8**.

Exercise 4 – Using Associativity

This exercise uses a process called associativity. Associativity is a feature of Mastercam that links the geometry with toolpath parameters to create a complete operation. This means that when you change any part of an operation, such as changing the geometry, you can regenerate the toolpath. The operation(s) for each toolpath are generated in the Operations Manager.

In this exercise, you make a design change to the part by changing the 3/8" fillets to ¼" fillets. After you make the design change, you update the toolpath and change the tool from a ½" endmill to a 3/8"endmill.

This exercise shows you how to use the following functions to make changes to the design and the toolpath.
- ◆ **Delete**
- ◆ **Operations Manager**
- ◆ **Toolpath parameters**
- ◆ **Regenerating the toolpath**

▶ *Modify the geometry*

1. Open **elbow.mc8**.

2. Choose
- ◆ **MAIN MENU**
- ◆ **Delete**

3. Select the .375 inch fillet at position 1.

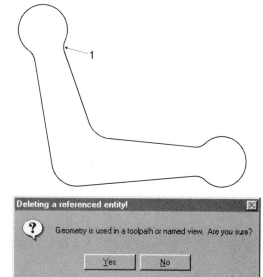

4. When the prompt shown at right appears, choose Yes.

Note: To avoid getting messages like the "Are you sure?" message shown in the picture above, choose MAIN MENU, Screen, Configure to display the System Configuration dialog box. Choose the NC Settings tab and select "Suppress associativity warning messages."

5. Delete the remaining fillets, as shown at right.

6. Create .25 fillets at the positions where you just deleted the .375 fillets. Use the techniques you learned in Exercise 1.

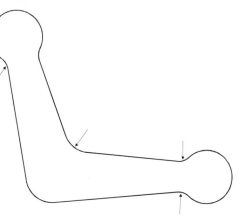

▶ Select a different tool for the toolpath

1. Press [Alt+O] to open the Operations Manager.

2. Choose the **Parameters** icon.

```
⊟ ✗ Toolpath Group #1
   ⊟ 🦑 1 - Contour
      ─ 📋 Parameters
      ─ 🔩 #1 - 0.5000 ENDMILL1 FLAT - 1/2
      ─ 📷 Geometry - (1) chain(s)
      ─ 🏭 D:\MILL8\NCI\ELBOW.NCI - 0.0K
```

3. Select a 3/8" flat endmill from the tool library.

4. Choose
   ◆ **OK**
   ◆ **Regen Path**
   ◆ **OK**

5. Save the file as **elbow1.mc8**.

3 *Modifying a 2D Contour Toolpath*

This chapter describes how to make changes to the toolpath you created in Chapter 2. It also shows you how to add a chamfer to the contour toolpath and create a mirror image of the part and toolpath.

Exercise 1 – Adding Roughing and Finishing Passes

You decided that the toolpath you created in Chapter 2 machines too much stock in one pass. In this exercise you will change tools and add roughing and finishing passes. The final toolpath for this exercise should look like the picture below. You will:

◆ **Use the Operations Manager**
◆ **Change toolpath parameters**
◆ **Add a new tool**
◆ **Copy an operation**

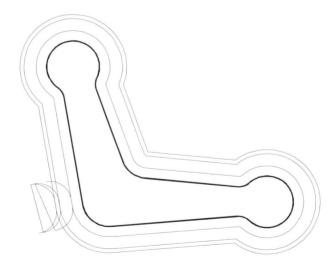

▶ *Open the file*

1. Open **elbow1.mc8**.

2. Choose
   - ◆ **MAIN MENU**
   - ◆ **Toolpaths**
   - ◆ **Operations**

Note: You can also open the Operations Manager by pressing [Alt + O].

▶ *Make a copy of the contour toolpath*

1. Right-click on the **Contour** folder icon.

2. While holding the right mouse button down, drag the Contour folder icon beneath the NCI icon.

3. Release the mouse button. The menu shown on the right displays.

4. Choose **Copy after**. The Operations Manager shows two operations as shown in the picture on the right.

▶ *Change the first toolpath to contour roughing*

1. Choose the **Parameters** icon for the first contour toolpath.

2. Right-click in the tool display area and select a 1" flat endmill.

3. Select the **Contour parameters** tab.

4. Set the **Depth** parameter to **-.25**

5. Set the **XY stock to leave** parameter to **.04**

6. Select the **Multi passes** check box and choose the **Multi passes** button.

7. Enter the values as shown on the dialog box at right.

8. Choose **OK**.

Multi Passes

Roughing passes

Number: 2

Spacing: 0.1

Finishing passes

Number: 0

Spacing: 0.01

Machine finish passes at

○ Final depth   ● All depths

☑ Keep tool down

OK   Cancel   Help

9. Choose the **Lead in/out** button.

10. Enter the values shown on the following dialog box.

Lead In/Out

☐ Enter/exit at midpoint in closed contours   Overlap: 0.2

☑ Entry
  Line
    ○ Perpendicular ● Tangent
    Length: 0.0 % 0.0
    Ramp height: 0.0
  Arc
    Radius: 50.0 % 0.5
    Sweep: 90.0
    Helix height: 0.0
  ☐ Use entry point
  ☐ Use point depth
  ☐ Enter on first depth cut only

☑ Exit
  Line
    ○ Perpendicular ● Tangent
    Length: 0.0 % 0.0
    Ramp height: 0.0
  Arc
    Radius: 50.0 % 0.5
    Sweep: 90.0
    Helix height: 0.0
  ☐ Use exit point
  ☐ Use point depth
  ☐ Exit on last depth cut only

OK   Cancel   Help

11. Choose **OK** twice.

▶ *Change the second toolpath to contour finishing*

1. Choose the **Parameters** icon for the second operation.

2. Choose the **Contour parameters** tab.

3. Set the **Depth** parameter to **-.25**

4. Set the **XY stock to leave** parameter to **0**

5. Choose **OK**.

6. Choose
   - ◆ **Select All**
   - ◆ **Regen Path**

> Tip: The blue check mark over the Contour folder icon for the second operation means only that operation is selected. You must have both operations selected before you can regenerate the complete set of operations.

7. Choose **OK**. The finished toolpath should look like the following picture.

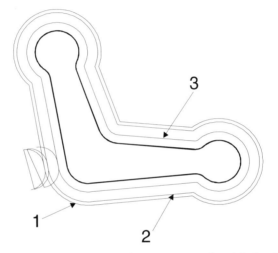

Note: Position 1 points to the first roughing pass made with the 1" endmill. Position 2 indicates the second roughing pass made with the 1" endmill, and position 3 points to the finish pass made with the ½" endmill.

▶ *Backplot to view the toolpath*

1. Choose **Backplot**.

2. Set the **Verify** option to **Y** (Yes).

3. Choose **Step** repeatedly to backplot the toolpath.

4. Save as **elbow2.mc8**.

Exercise 2 – Creating a Contour Chamfer

You need to change the tool and add a contour chamfer to the finishing pass of the part. A chamfer is a beveled edge; you can specify the width and depth of the chamfer. This exercise shows you how to use the following functions:

◆ **Operations Manager**
◆ **2D contour chamfer**

▶ *Set chamfering parameters*

1. Choose
   ◆ **MAIN MENU**
   ◆ **Toolpaths**
   ◆ **Operations**

2. Choose the **Parameters** icon of the second contour toolpath.

3. Select the 1" chamfer mill tool.

4. Choose the **Contour parameters** tab.

5. Set the contour type to **2D Chamfer** and choose the **Chamfer** button.

6. Enter the values shown on the following dialog box.

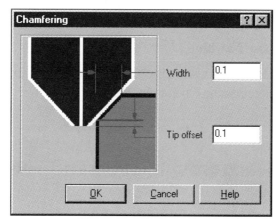

7. Choose **OK** twice.

8. Choose **Regen Path**.

9. Choose **Verify**. The Verify toolbar opens.

10. Choose **Configure**.

11. Enter the values shown on the following dialog box.

12. Choose **OK**.

13. Choose **Machine**.

14. Once the verification is complete, close the Verify toolbar and choose **OK** to close the Operations Manager.

15. Save the file.

Exercise 3 – Mirroring the Part and Toolpath

You are required to manufacture both left-hand and right-hand versions of the part. You can do this by mirroring the part and the toolpath. Mirroring the toolpath lets you maintain the original toolpath parameters and machining direction, ensuring that the duplicated part has the identical finish and size as the original.

This exercise shows you how to use the following function:

◆ **Toolpaths, Next Menu, Transform, Mirror**

▶ *Open the file*

1. Open **elbow2.mc8**.

2. Press [Alt + F2] to unzoom the geometry.

3. Use the keyboard arrow keys to position the part in the far right corner of the graphics window.

4. Press [F9] to display the construction origin.

▶ *Transform and mirror the toolpath*

1. Choose

◆ **MAIN MENU**
◆ **Toolpaths**
◆ **Next menu**
◆ **Transform**

2. Enter the values shown on the following dialog box.

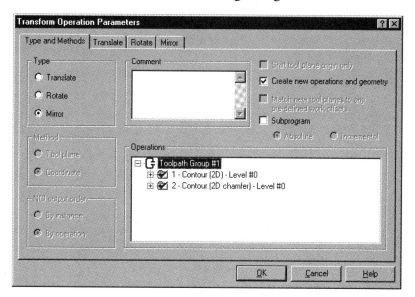

Note: In the Operations list area, select the Toolpath Group icon to make sure you have both operations selected.

3. Choose the **Mirror** tab.

4. Enter the values shown on the following dialog box.

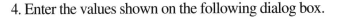

5. Choose **OK**. The part should look like the following picture.

Note: The arrows show the cutter direction.

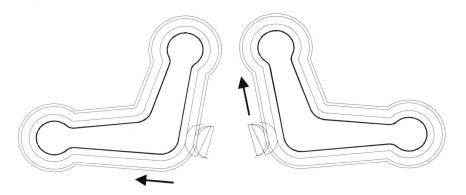

Note: In the original toolpath on the right, the cutter is climb milling. Selecting the Reverse toolpath option in the Mirror parameters dialog box ensures that climb milling is also done on the mirrored part. Milling the parts without reversing the toolpath would possibly result in variations in finish and size.

6. Save the file.

The following picture shows the complete set of toolpaths in the Operations Manager.

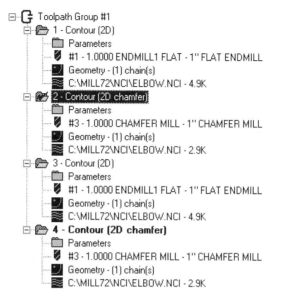

Note: To help you identify each operation, you can add a comment to it in the Tool parameters dialog as shown below. You can add or edit comments without regenerating the toolpath.

4 *Rotating 2D Geometry and Contour Toolpath*

This chapter shows you how to use the Rotate and Transform functions to create a 2D part and contour toolpath. In the first exercise, you create the part and learn how to rotate geometry. In the second exercise, you create the toolpath for the part. Exercise 3 shows you how to rotate a toolpath using the Transform, Rotate toolpath.

Exercise 1 – Creating the Geometry

This exercise shows you how to use the following functions to create the part, a wheel with three symmetrical slots, shown in the following picture. You will:

- ◆ **Create arcs, tangent arcs, and lines**
- ◆ **Use the Xform, Rotate function**
- ◆ **Use the Modify, Trim function**

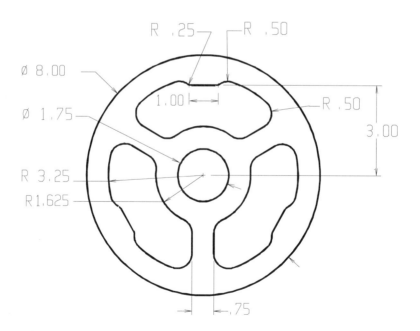

▶ *Create the inner and outer circles*

1. Choose
   - ◆ **MAIN MENU**
   - ◆ **Create**
   - ◆ **Arc**
   - ◆ **Circ pt+dia**

2. *Enter the diameter.* **8**

> Tip: Remember that the values display in the prompt area as you type.

3. *Enter the center point.* **0,0**

4. Press [Esc] and reselect **Circ pt+dia**

5. *Enter the diameter.* **1.75**

6. *Enter the center point.* **0,0**

7. Press [Esc] to exit the circle function.

8. Right-click in the graphics window.

9. Choose **Fit screen** from the right-click menu.

▶ *Create the construction lines*

To construct the symmetrical slots, begin by defining two edges.

1. Choose
   - ◆ **MAIN MENU**
   - ◆ **Create**
   - ◆ **Line**
   - ◆ **Vertical**

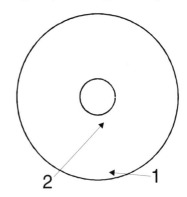

2. Select at position 1 then at position 2 to draw the construction line.

3. *Enter the X coordinate.* **.375**

4. Create another vertical line to the left of the first line by selecting next to position one and then next to position two.

5. *Enter the X coordinate.* **-.375**
The part should look like the
picture shown on the right.

(The lines represent the edges of
two slots and will be used in
constructing the position of all
three slots in the part. Refer to
the drawing on page 43.)

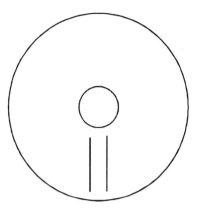

 Rotate the vertical construction line
Start creating the first slot by defining two lines.

1. Choose
   ◆ **MAIN MENU**
   ◆ **Xform**
   ◆ **Rotate**

2. Select the left vertical line. It is highlighted in white.

3. Choose
   ◆ **Done**
   ◆ **Origin**

4. Enter the values shown on
   the dialog box to the right.

5. Choose **OK**. The part
   should look like the
   following picture.

The first slot is taking shape.

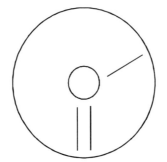

 Create the inner and outer arcs

Create the inner and outer curves of the first slot in the wheel.

1. Choose
   - ◆ **MAIN MENU**
   - ◆ **Create**
   - ◆ **Arc**
   - ◆ **Polar**
   - ◆ **Sketch**

2. *Enter the center point.* **0,0**

3. *Enter the radius.* **3.25**

> Tip: Position the cursor over the perimeter of either circle. Mastercam displays a square at the center, which is 0,0.

4. Draw the initial angle at position 1 and the final angle at position 2.

Note: Mastercam creates all arcs in a counterclockwise direction.

5. *Enter the center point.* **0,0**

6. *Enter the radius.* **1.625**

7. Sketch the initial angle at position 3 and the final angle at position 4. The part should look like the following picture.

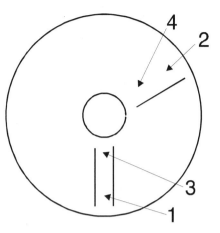

Tip: Save your file as wheel.mc8 if your part looks like this. Hereafter, you can auto-save the file by pressing the keyboard shortcut [Alt + A].

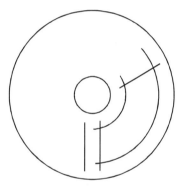

▶ **Create four ½ inch fillets**

Use what you learned in Chapter 2 to create four ½" fillets. When you have created the fillets, the part should look like the following picture.

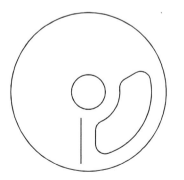

▶ ***Create the 1 inch horizontal line***

You create this line first in the horizontal position because you know its position and length. You then use the Rotate function to rotate it down into the slot to create the flat area on the back side of the slot.

1. Choose
   - ◆ **MAIN MENU**
   - ◆ **Create**
   - ◆ **Line**
   - ◆ **Endpoints**

2. *Specify the first endpoint.* **–.5,3**

3. *Specify the second endpoint* **.5,3**. The part should look like the following picture.

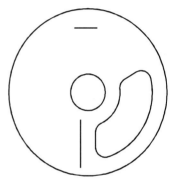

Tip: You can auto-save the file at this point by pressing [Alt + A]. Select the Active option and name the file **wheel.mc8**.

▶ ***Rotate the 1 inch horizontal line down to the slot***

1. Choose
   - ◆ **MAIN MENU**
   - ◆ **Xform**
   - ◆ **Rotate**

2. Select the 1 inch horizontal line.

3. Choose
   - ◆ **Done**
   - ◆ **Origin**

4. Enter the values as shown on the dialog box at right.

5. Choose **OK**. The part should look like the following picture.

Tip: if you make a mistake, open the previous version of the file.

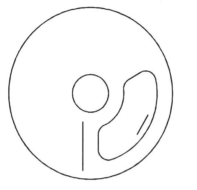

▶ *Create the tangent arcs*

1. Choose
   - ◆ **MAIN MENU**
   - ◆ **Create**
   - ◆ **Arc**
   - ◆ **Tangent**
   - ◆ **Point**

2. Select the arc at position 1.

3. Select the endpoint of the line at position 2.

4. *Enter the radius.* **.5**

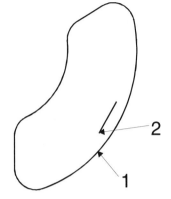

5. Select the arc to keep at position 1.

6. Repeat steps 2 through 5 to create the arc at the other end of the line.

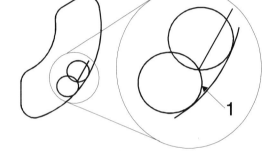

▶ ***Trim the arcs and delete the construction line***

1. Choose
    ◆ **MAIN MENU**
    ◆ **Modify**
    ◆ **Trim**
    ◆ **Divide**

2. Select the arcs at positions 1, 2, and 3 in that order.

3. Delete the vertical construction line to the left of the slot. The part should look like the following picture.

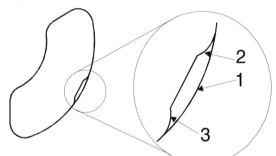

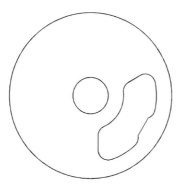

 Copy and rotate the slot to create the remaining slots

1. Choose
   - ◆ **MAIN MENU**
   - ◆ **Xform**
   - ◆ **Rotate**
   - ◆ **Chain**

2. Select anywhere on the slot.

3. Choose
   - ◆ **Done** twice
   - ◆ **Origin**

4. Enter the values shown on the dialog box at right.

5. Choose **Done**. The part should look like the following picture.

Rotate

Operation
- ○ Move
- ⦿ Copy
- ○ Join

☐ Use construction attributes

Number of steps: `2`

Rotation angle: `120.0`

| OK | Cancel | Help |

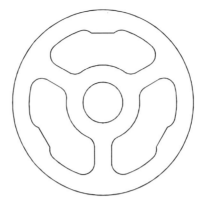

6. Save the file as **wheel.mc8**.

Exercise 2 – Create the Toolpath

This exercise shows you how to use the following functions to create a toolpath for one of the slots and add the toolpath to the remaining slots. The final toolpath for this exercise should look like the following picture. You will:

◆ **Use Toolpaths, Contour**
◆ **Use chaining**
◆ **Use tool and contour parameters**
◆ **Use the Chain Manager**

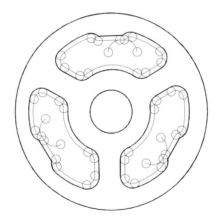

▶ ***Open the file***

1. Open **wheel.mc8**.

2. Choose
   - ◆ **MAIN MENU**
   - ◆ **Toolpaths**
   - ◆ **Contour**

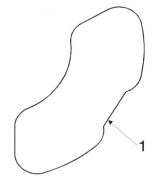

3. Save the NCI file as **wheel.nci**.

▶ ***Chain the toolpath***

1. Select the start point for the chain at position 1.

2. Choose **Done**.

3. Right-click in the tool display area and select a 3/8" flat endmill from the tool library.

4. Select the **Contour parameters** tab.

5. Select the **Lead In/Out** check box and choose the **Lead in/out** button.

6. Enter the values shown on the following dialog box.

Lead In/Out		? X
☐ Enter/exit at midpoint in closed contours	Overlap	0.2

☑ **Entry**

Line
- ○ Perpendicular ◉ Tangent
- Length: 0.0 % 0.0
- Ramp height: 0.0

Arc
- Radius: 133.33333 % 0.5
- Sweep: 90.0
- Helix height: 0.0

- ☐ Use entry point
- ☐ Use point depth
- ☐ Enter on first depth cut only

☑ **Exit**

Line
- ○ Perpendicular ◉ Tangent
- Length: 0.0 % 0.0
- Ramp height: 0.0

Arc
- Radius: 133.33333 % 0.5
- Sweep: 90.0
- Helix height: 0.0

- ☐ Use exit point
- ☐ Use point depth
- ☐ Exit on last depth cut only

OK   Cancel   Help

Note: The line length and arc radius may be entered as a percentage of the tool diameter or as a distance.

7. Choose **OK** twice. The toolpath should look like the following picture.

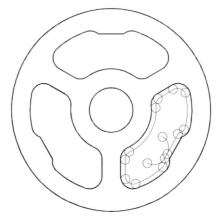

Note: You can create a toolpath for all three contours individually, but in the following procedure you learn how to use the Chain Manager to add the chain and the toolpath to the remaining slots.

▶ *Add the toolpath to the remaining slots*

1. Choose **Operations**.

2. Select the **Geometry** icon. The Chain Manager dialog box displays.

3. Right-click on **Chain 1**. The right-click menu displays as shown in the picture on the right.

4. Choose **Add chain**.

5. Chain the remaining contours using the method you used to chain the first contour.

Note: Make sure all the chains start at the same place and are going in the same direction.

6. Choose **Done**. The Chain
   Manager displays the chains for
   all three contours, as shown at
   right.

7. Choose
   - ◆ **OK**
   - ◆ **Regen Path**

8. When the Toolpath generation
   complete dialog box displays,
   choose **OK**. The toolpath should
   look like the following picture.

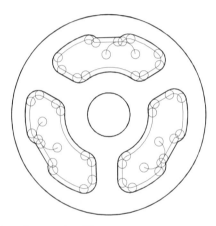

9. Choose **OK** and save the file.

Exercise 3 – Rotating a Toolpath

The part shown in the following picture has 30 identical contours. Chaining
each contour individually would be time-consuming. In this exercise, you chain
one of the contours and then use the following functions to rotate the toolpath
around the part.

- ◆ **Toolpaths, Contour**
- ◆ **Chaining**
- ◆ **Tool and contour parameters**
- ◆ **Transform, Rotate**

 ### *Open and save the file*

1. Open **rotation.mc8**.

2. Save the file as **rotation1.mc8**.

 ### *Choose a toolpath type and chain the toolpath*

1. Choose
   - ◆ **MAIN MENU**
   - ◆ **Toolpaths**
   - ◆ **Contour**

2. Save the NCI file as **rotation1.nci**.

3. Select the start point of the chain at position 1.

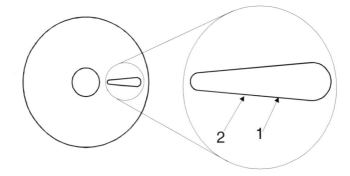

Note: The geometry has been broken at position 2 to allow you to start the chain there. Starting the toolpath at this position allows room for tool entry and exit.

4. Choose **Done**.

5. Access the tool library and select a ¼" flat endmill.

6. Select the **Contour parameters** tab.

7. Select the **Multi passes** check box and choose the **Multi passes** button.

8. Enter the values shown on the following dialog box.

Multi Passes	? ✕
Roughing passes	
Number	1
Spacing	0.065
Finishing passes	
Number	1
Spacing	0.06
Machine finish passes at	
○ Final depth	◉ All depths
☑ Keep tool down	
OK	Cancel	Help

9. Choose **OK**.

10. Select the **Lead in/out** check box and choose the **Lead in/out** button.

11. Enter the values shown on the following dialog box.

Lead In/Out

☐ Enter/exit at midpoint in closed contours   Overlap   [0.0]

☑ **Entry**
    Line
      ○ Perpendicular   ● Tangent
      Length: [0.0]   % [0.0]
      Ramp height: [0.0]

    Arc
      Radius: [40.0]   % [0.1]
      Sweep: [45.0]
      Helix height: [0.0]

    ☐ Use entry point
    ☐ Use point depth
    ☐ Enter on first depth cut only

☑ **Exit**
    Line
      ○ Perpendicular   ● Tangent
      Length: [0.0]   % [0.0]
      Ramp height: [0.0]

    Arc
      Radius: [40.0]   % [0.1]
      Sweep: [45.0]
      Helix height: [0.0]

    ☐ Use exit point
    ☐ Use point depth
    ☐ Exit on last depth cut only

[OK]   [Cancel]   [Help]

12. Choose **OK** twice. The toolpath should look like the following picture.

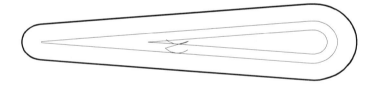

▶ *Rotate the toolpath*

1. Choose
    ◆ **Next menu**
    ◆ **Transform**

2. Enter the values shown on the following dialog box.

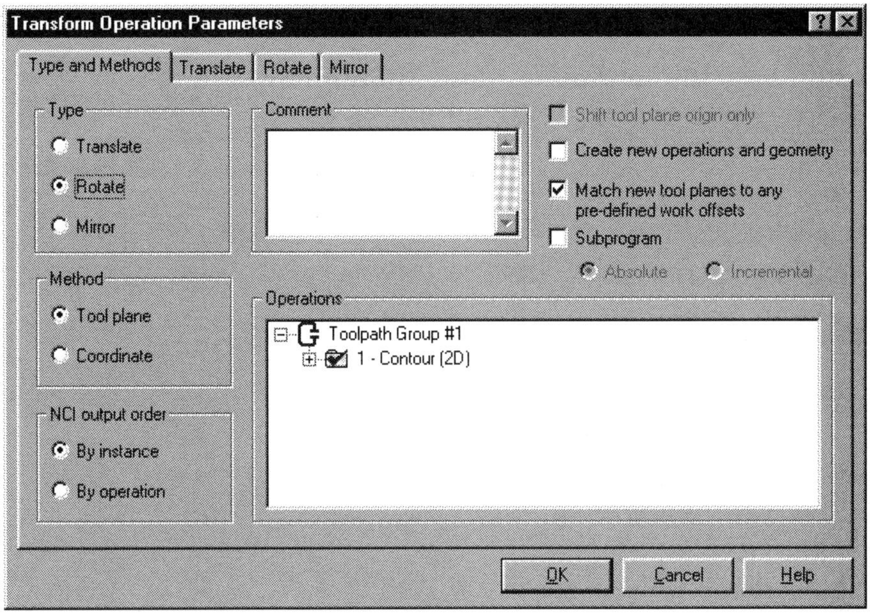

3. Select the **Rotate** tab.

4. Enter the values shown on the following dialog box.

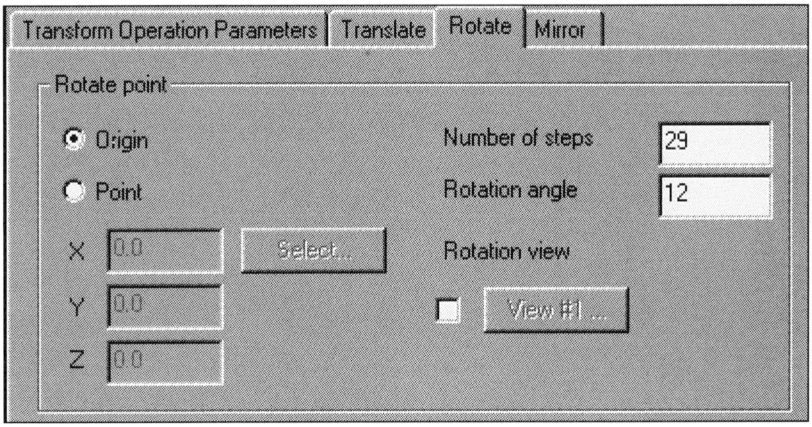

5. Choose **OK**. The toolpath should look like the following picture.

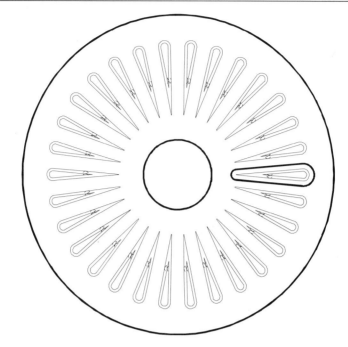

6. Press [Alt + O] to open the Operations Manager.

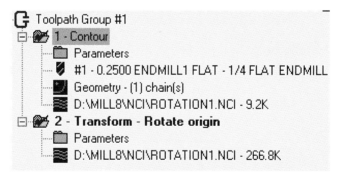

Note: The Operations Manager shows that there are only two operations: the original Contour operation and the new Transform, Rotate operation. Rotating the toolpath using this method is very efficient, but you cannot modify just one toolpath in the operation.

7. Save the file.

Exercise 4 – Creating New Operations

This exercise shows you how to use the following function to rotate the cutout around the part and create a separate toolpath operation for each cutout. You will:

◆ **Use Toolpaths, Transform, Rotate**

▶ *Open the file and access the Transform toolpath parameters*

1. Open **rotation1.mc8**.

2. Choose
   ◆ **MAIN MENU**
   ◆ **Toolpaths**
   ◆ **Operations**

3. Select the **Parameters** icon for the Transform, Rotate toolpath.

4. Enter the values shown on the following dialog box.

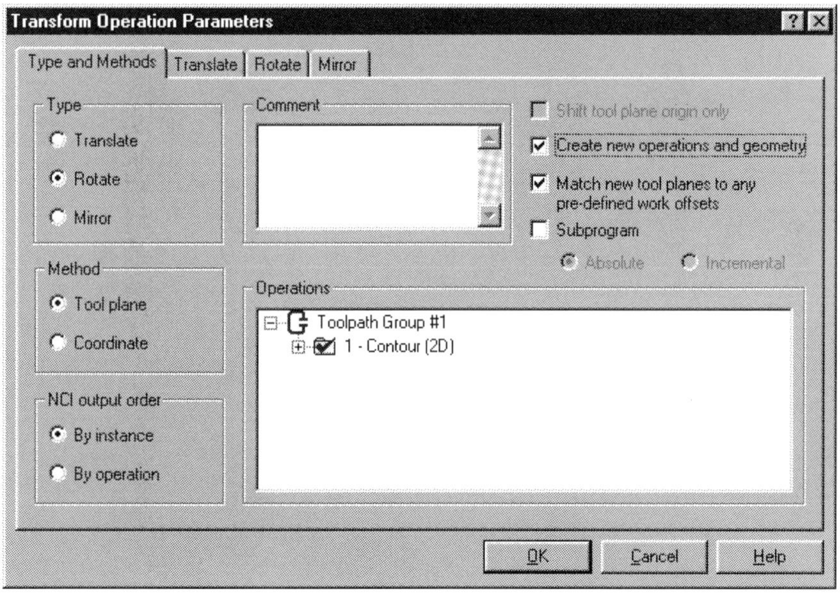

Note: Make sure to select the Create new operations and geometry check box.

5. Choose **OK**.

6. Choose
   ◆ **Select All**
   ◆ **Regen Path**

7. Choose **OK**. The toolpath should look like the following picture.

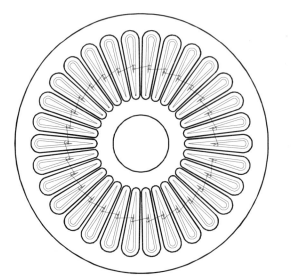

Note: The Operations Manager shows a total of 30 cutouts and contour toolpaths. You can now modify the parameters of each cutout and contour toolpath individually without affecting the other 29 cutouts or contour toolpaths.

- 27 - Contour (2D)
  - Parameters
  - #1 - 0.2500 ENDMILL1 FLAT - 1/4 FLAT ENDMILL
  - Geometry - (1) chain(s)
  - C:\MILL72\NCI\ROTATION1.NCI - 4.5K
- 28 - Contour (2D)
  - Parameters
  - #1 - 0.2500 ENDMILL1 FLAT - 1/4 FLAT ENDMILL
  - Geometry - (1) chain(s)
  - C:\MILL72\NCI\ROTATION1.NCI - 4.5K
- 29 - Contour (2D)
  - Parameters
  - #1 - 0.2500 ENDMILL1 FLAT - 1/4 FLAT ENDMILL
  - Geometry - (1) chain(s)
  - C:\MILL72\NCI\ROTATION1.NCI - 4.5K
- **30 - Contour (2D)**
  - Parameters
  - #1 - 0.2500 ENDMILL1 FLAT - 1/4 FLAT ENDMILL
  - Geometry - (1) chain(s)
  - C:\MILL72\NCI\ROTATION1.NCI - 4.5K

5 Making a 3D Wireframe Design and 3D Contour Toolpath

This chapter guides you through the design of a 3D wireframe part and the creation of a 3D contour toolpath for the part.

Exercise 1 – Creating the Geometry

This exercise shows you how to use the following functions to create the part outline shown in the following shaded picture.

- ◆ **Creating arcs and lines**
- ◆ **Filleting**
- ◆ **Trimming**
- ◆ **Construction planes**
- ◆ **Mirroring**

The following pictures show the dimensions of the part outline.

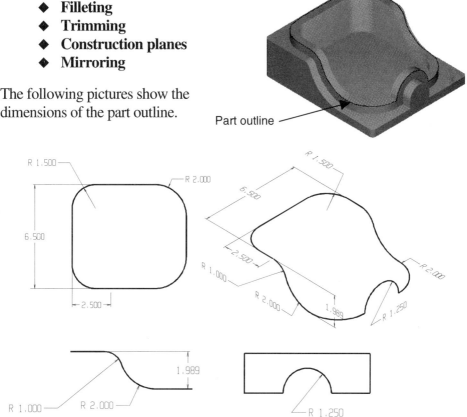

Part outline

▶ *Create the horizontal and vertical construction lines*

1. Choose
   - ◆ **MAIN MENU**
   - ◆ **Create**
   - ◆ **Line**
   - ◆ **Horizontal**

2. Draw the line at position 1.

> Tip: To make sure you sketch the lines in the correct location, press [F9] to display the construction origin (0,0).

3. *Enter the y coordinate.* **-3.25**

4. Draw the line at position 2.

5. *Enter the y coordinate.* **0**

6. Choose
   - ◆ **Backup**
   - ◆ **Vertical**

7. Draw the line at position 3.

8. *Enter the x coordinate.* **0**

9. Draw the line at position 4.

10. *Enter the x coordinate.* **2.5**

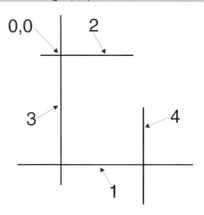

▶ *Trim the lines*

1. Choose
   - ◆ **MAIN MENU**
   - ◆ **Modify**
   - ◆ **Trim**
   - ◆ **1 entity**

2. Select the lines at positions 1, 2, 3, and 4 in that order.

3. Delete the lines at positions 5 and 6. The part should look like the following picture.

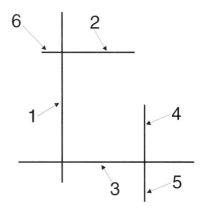

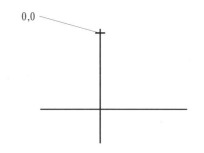

0,0

▶ *Create the 1.5 inch fillet*

Use what you learned in the previous chapters to create the 1.5 inch fillet. When you have created the 1.5 fillet, the part should look like the following picture.

Note: If you do not remember how to create the fillet, see Exercise 2 in Chapter 1 for detailed instructions.

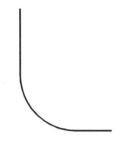

▶ *Create the arc*

1. Set the Gview to **I** (Isometric) and Cplane to **F** (Front).

2. Choose the **Z** button on the Secondary Menu.

3. Select the line endpoint at position 1.

Note: The Z depth is now set to 3.25.

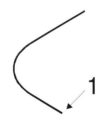

4. Choose
   - ◆ **MAIN MENU**
   - ◆ **Create**
   - ◆ **Arc**
   - ◆ **Tangent**
   - ◆ **1 entity**

5. Select the line at position 1.

6. Select the line endpoint at position 2.

7. *Enter the radius.* **1**

8. Select the arc to keep. The part should look like the following picture.

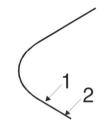

▶ **Create the construction line**

Note: The construction line is used to create a 2 inch arc tangent to the 1 inch arc.

1. Choose
   - ◆ **MAIN MENU**
   - ◆ **Create**
   - ◆ **Line**
   - ◆ **Horizontal**

2. Draw the line at position 1.

3. *Enter the y coordinate.* **–1.989**

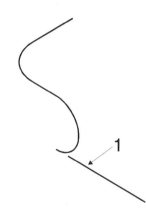

▶ **Create a fillet tangent to the arc and the construction line**

1. Choose
   - ◆ **MAIN MENU**
   - ◆ **Create**
   - ◆ **Fillet**
   - ◆ **Radius**

2. *Enter the fillet radius.* **2**

3. Select the arc at position 1.

4. Select the line at position 2.

5. Select the fillet to use. The part should look like the following picture.

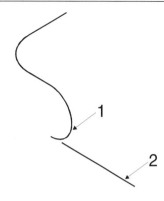

▶ **Create a 2 inch arc tangent to the fillet endpoint**

1. Set the Cplane to **T** (Top).

2. Choose the **Z** button on the Secondary Menu.

3. Select the fillet endpoint at position 1 to set the Z depth to –1.989.

Note: Position 1 is the end of the arc.

4. Choose
   - ◆ **MAIN MENU**
   - ◆ **Create**
   - ◆ **Arc**
   - ◆ **Polar**
   - ◆ **Start pt**

5. Select the fillet endpoint again at position 1, which is at the end of the arc.

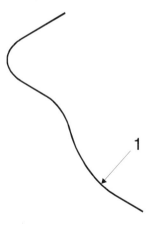

6. *Enter the radius.* **2**

7. *Enter the initial angle.* **270**

8. *Enter the final angle.* **0** The part should look like the picture shown on the right.

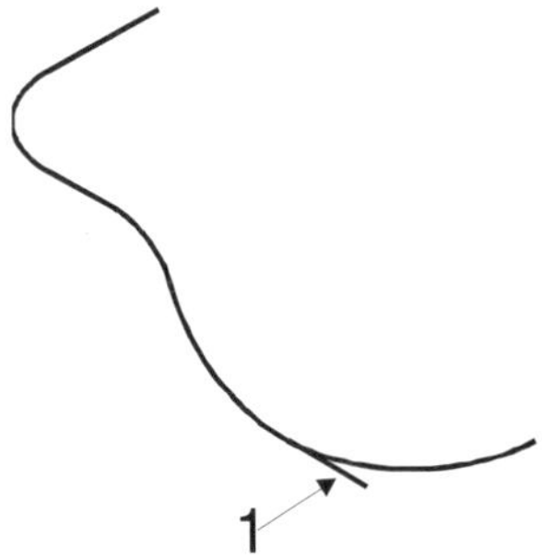

9. Delete the line at position 1. The part should look like the following picture.

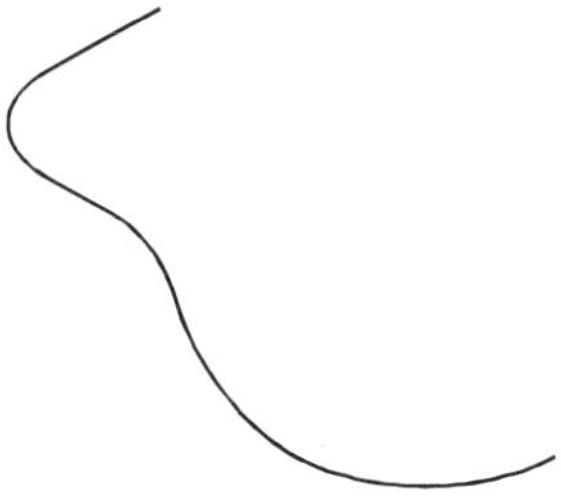

▶ *Create the 1.25 radius arc in the side construction plane*

1. Set the Cplane to **S** (Side).

2. Choose the **Z** button on the Secondary Menu.

3. Select the endpoint of the arc at position 1 to set the Z depth at 7.3245.

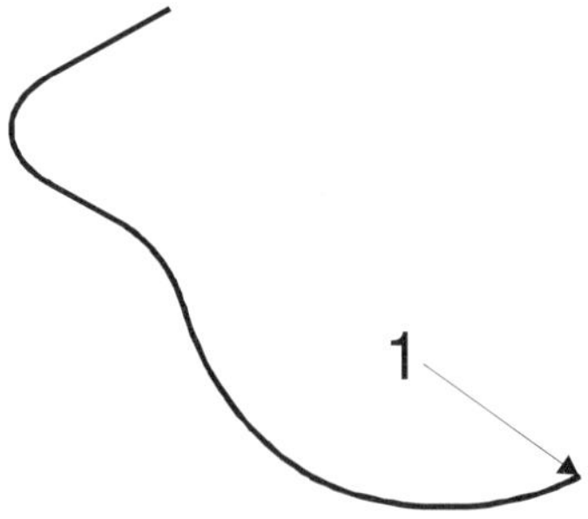

4. Choose
   ◆ **MAIN MENU**
   ◆ **Create**
   ◆ **Arc**
   ◆ **Polar**
   ◆ **End pt**

5. Select the endpoint of the arc at position 1.

6. *Enter the radius.* **1.25**

7. *Enter the initial angle.* **0**

8. *Enter the final angle.* **180** The part should look like the following picture.

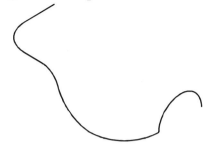

▶ *Mirror the entities*

Note: Now that you have created half of the part, use the Mirror function to create the other half.

1. Set the Cplane to **T** (Top).

2. Choose
   - ◆ **MAIN MENU**
   - ◆ **Xform**
   - ◆ **Mirror**
   - ◆ **Chain**
   - ◆ **Partial**

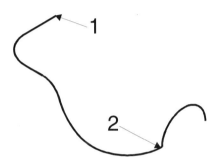

3. Select the chain at position 1.

4. Select the end of the chain at position 2.

5. Choose
   - ◆ **Done** twice
   - ◆ **X axis**

6. Enter the values shown on the following dialog box.

7. Choose **OK**. The final part should look like the following picture.

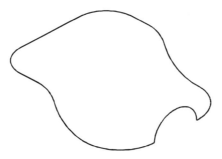

8. Save the file as **3Dcontour.mc8**.

Exercise 2 – Creating the Contour Toolpath

This exercise shows you how to use the following functions to create a contour toolpath for the part you designed in Exercise 1. When you finish this exercise, the toolpath should look like the picture on the next page. You will:

◆ **Use Toolpaths, Contour**
◆ **Use Chain**
◆ **Create Tool and contour parameters**
◆ **Apply Lead In/Out parameters**
◆ **Use Incremental depth**

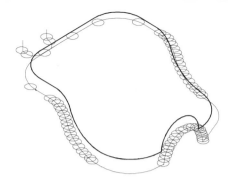

 ### Open the file and choose a toolpath type

1. Open **3Dcontour.mc8**.

2. Choose
   - ◆ **MAIN MENU**
   - ◆ **Toolpaths**
   - ◆ **Contour**

3. Save the NCI file as **3Dcontour.nci**.

Chain the toolpath

1. Choose **Chain**.

2. Select at position 1 to start the chain.

3. Choose **Done**.

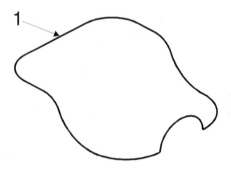

Select the tool and enter the contour parameters

1. Access the tool library and select a ½" flat endmill.

2. Select the **Contour parameters** tab.

3. Enter the values shown on the following dialog box.

Note: The Depth parameter is automatically set to Incremental so that the tool follows the Z motion of the contour.

4. Select the **Lead in/out** check box and choose the **Lead in/out** button.

5. Enter the values shown on the following dialog box.

6. Choose **OK** twice. The completed toolpath should look like the following picture.

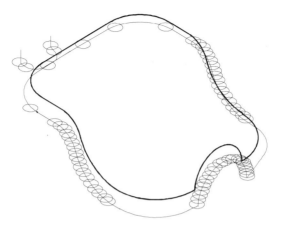

6 *Creating Drill Toolpaths*

Mastercam includes several types of drill toolpaths. The first exercise in this chapter teaches you how to make arcs and create a simple drill toolpath for a part. The second exercise shows you how to modify the geometry from Exercise 1. The third exercise involves programming a drill toolpath at multiple Z depths.

Exercise 1 – Creating Arcs and a Drill Toolpath

The following picture shows the dimensions for the part used in this exercise. In this exercise, you will:

- ◆ **Use Create, Arc**
- ◆ **Use Mask on arc**
- ◆ **Use Drill point sorting options**
- ◆ **Use Toolpaths, Drill**

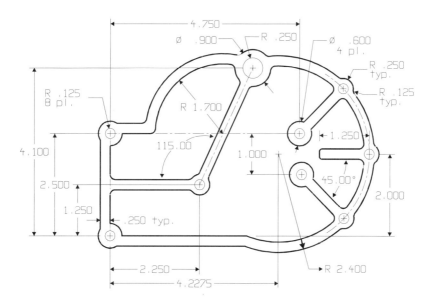

▶ *Open the file*

1. Open **gasket.mc8**.

2. Choose the **Gview (Top)** button from the toolbar to change the graphics view to Top.

3. Choose the **Fit** button from the toolbar to fit the geometry in the graphics window.

▶ *Create arcs to represent the drill holes*

1. Choose
   - ◆ **MAIN MENU**
   - ◆ **Create**
   - ◆ **Arc**
   - ◆ **Circ pt+dia**

2. *Enter the diameter.* **.25**

3. *Enter the center point.* Press the letter [C] on the keyboard to make sure you select the center point of the arcs.

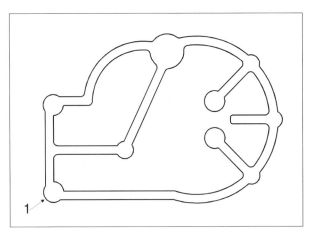

4. Select the arc marked 1.

5. Repeat steps 2 through 4 for the remaining eight arcs shown in the following picture.

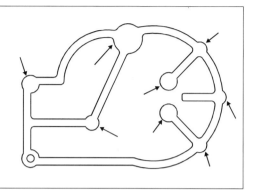

Tip: To avoid having to press [C] each time, turn the AutoCursor off using the right-click menu in the graphics window.

Your part should now look like the following picture:

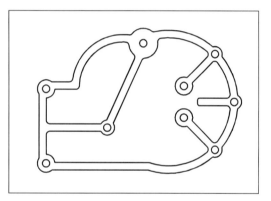

The next step is to create the toolpath for this geometry.

▶ *Choose arcs for the drill toolpath*

1. Choose
   - ◆ **MAIN MENU**
   - ◆ **Toolpaths**
   - ◆ **Drill**

2. Save the NCI file as **gasket.nci**.

3. Choose **Mask on arc**.

4. Select one of the .250 diameter holes.

5. *Enter arc radius matching tolerance.* Use the default value and press [Enter].

6. Choose
   ◆ **Window**
   ◆ **Inside**

7. Click on the upper left corner of the stock, drag, and click on the lower right corner of the stock to select the window.

8. Choose **Done**. The system selects all the .250 diameter holes.

9. Choose **Options**.

10. Choose the **Point to Point** sorting button from the dialog box.

Tip: The order of drill points for this part is not efficient, so you need to sort the points in a more logical order.

11. Choose **OK**.

12. *Select sorting start point*. Select the arc in the bottom left corner.

13. Choose **Done**. The toolpath with the points sorted should look like the picture shown on the right:

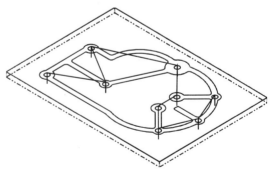

▶ *Enter the tool parameters*

1. Right-click in the tool display area.

2. Choose **Get tool from library**.

3. Choose the **Filter** button.

4. In the Tool Types section, choose the **None** button. Then select the **Drill** button.

Note: The tool filter makes it easier to choose the correct tool by showing you only the drills in the tool library.

Drill button

5. Choose **OK**.

6. Select the ¼" drill and choose **OK**.

▶ *Enter the drill parameters*

1. Select the **Simple drill – no peck** tab.

2. Enter the values shown on the following dialog box.

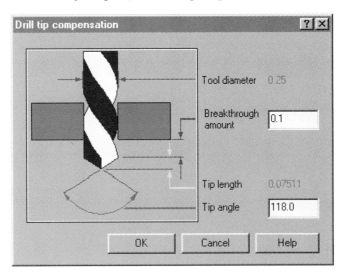

3. Choose the **Tip comp** button.

4. Enter the values shown on the Tip Compensation dialog box.

Note: These options set the breakthrough amount (how far the tool breaks through the bottom of the part) and the tip angle.

5. Choose **OK** twice. The resulting toolpath should look like the picture shown on the right:

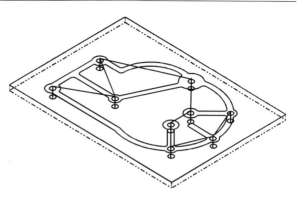

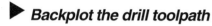 **Backplot the drill toolpath**

1. Choose
   ◆ **Operations**
   ◆ **Backplot**

2. Choose **Step** to move through the toolpath.

3. When the backplot is done, choose **OK**.

4. Choose **BACKUP**. The Operations Manager displays.

5. Choose **OK**.

Exercise 2 – Changing a Drill Hole

Your customer told you that one of the drill holes needs to have a .500 diameter instead of a .250 diameter. The easiest way to do this is to delete the hole from the original geometry and create a new toolpath for the modified hole using a larger tool. The final toolpath should look like the following picture:

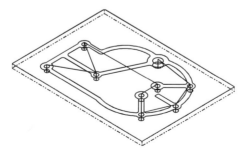

In this exercise, you will:
- ◆ **Use Delete**
- ◆ **Use Create, Arc**
- ◆ **Use Toolpaths, Drill**

▶ *Delete the .250 diameter hole*

1. Choose
   - ◆ **MAIN MENU**
   - ◆ **Delete**

2. Select the arc at position 1.

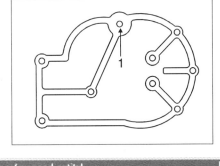

3. Choose **Yes** from the dialog box that displays.

4. Deleting a referenced entity!

   Geometry is used in a toolpath or named view. Are you sure?

   Yes   No

▶ *Create a new .500 diameter hole*

1. Choose
   - ◆ **MAIN MENU**
   - ◆ **Create**
   - ◆ **Arc**
   - ◆ **Circ pt+dia**

2. Create a .500 diameter hole where the .250 diameter hole used to be.

Note: In this case, Mastercam does not automatically adjust the drill toolpath to accommodate the change in the geometry. You have to create a new toolpath that fits the bigger hole.

▶ *Select the .500 diameter hole for a new drill toolpath*

1. Choose
   - ◆ **MAIN MENU**
   - ◆ **Toolpaths**
   - ◆ **Drill**
   - ◆ **Manual**

2. *Select points.* Select the center point of the .500 diameter hole and press [Esc].

3. *Select sorting start point.* Select the center point of the .500 diameter hole again.

4. Choose **Done**.

5. Select the .500 drill.

▶ *Enter the drill parameters*

1. Select the **Simple drill – no peck** tab.

2. Enter the values shown on the following dialog box.

Note: Do not change the Tip Comp settings. Mastercam automatically calculates a new tip comp for the .500 drill.

3. Choose **OK**.

▶ *Regenerate and backplot*

1. Choose **Operations**. You should see the following two toolpaths in the Operations Manager dialog box.

2. Choose **Regen Path**.

3. When the message shown on the right displays, choose **OK**.

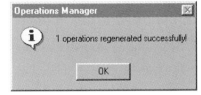

4. Choose
   ◆ **Select All**
   ◆ **Backplot**

5. Choose **Step** to move through the toolpath.

6. When the backplot is done, choose **OK**.

7. Choose **BACKUP**. The Operations Manager displays.

8. Choose **OK**. The completed toolpaths should look like the following picture:

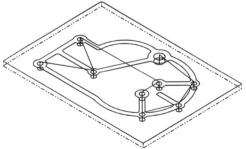

Exercise 3 - Drilling at Multiple Z Depths

Some parts require a drill toolpath at multiple Z depths. With Mastercam, you can use one selection to pick all the points, even if they lie at different Z depths. Also, using the Incremental option, you can apply the drill toolpath to multiple depths using just one set of parameters. The final toolpath for this exercise should look like the following picture:

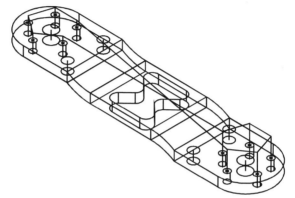

In this exercise, you learn how to:

- ◆ **Use the Window pts selection method**
- ◆ **Use Incremental drill heights**
- ◆ **Use Viewports**

▶ *Open the file and create the center drill toolpath*

1. Open **tab.mc8**.

2. Choose
   - ◆ **MAIN MENU**
   - ◆ **Toolpaths**
   - ◆ **Drill**

3. Save the NCI file as **tab.nci**.

4. Choose **Window pts**.

5. Click on the upper left corner of the stock, drag, and click on the lower right corner of the stock to draw a window that encloses the entire part.

6. *Select sorting start point.* Select the point at position 1 (the point turns red when you select it).

7. Choose **Done**.

8. Select the 1/8" center drill from the tool library.

9. Select the **Simple drill – no peck** tab.

10. Enter the values shown on the following dialog box.

Note: Using an absolute clearance value prevents gouging between the start point and the first drill point of the toolpath.

11. Choose **OK**.

▶ **Create the drill toolpath**

1. Choose **Operations**.

2. Right-click on the center drill toolpath and make a copy of it.

Note: If you do not remember how to copy a toolpath in the Operations Manager, see Exercise 1 in Chapter 3 for detailed instructions.

3. Choose the **Parameters** icon for the second toolpath.

4. Select the ¼" drill from the tool library.

5. Choose the **Simple drill – no peck** tab

6. Enter the values shown on the following dialog box.

7. Choose the **Tip comp** button.

8. Enter the values shown on the following dialog box.

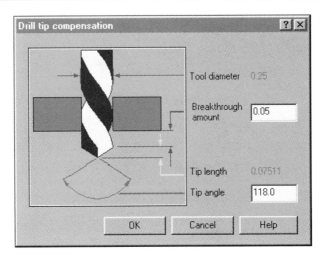

9. Choose **OK** twice.

▶ *Regenerate and backplot*

1. Choose
   - ◆ **Select All**
   - ◆ **Regen Path**
   - ◆ **OK**
   - ◆ **Backplot**

2. Press [Alt+W]. The Viewports dialog box opens.

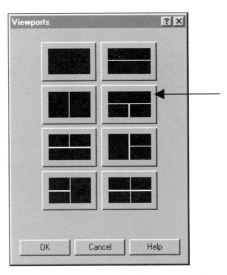

3. Choose the viewport button indicated by the arrow above and choose **OK**.

4. Backplot the toolpath using the **Step** function. You can see that the drill toolpaths are automatically adjusted to the multiple Z depths of the part. The final toolpaths should look like the following picture.

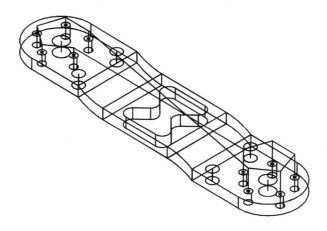

7 *Creating Facing and Pocket Toolpaths*

This chapter covers the basic concepts involved in creating pocket toolpaths. The first exercise focuses on using the Facing toolpath to clean off the top of the stock The second exercise uses different cutting methods on the same part for more effective cleanout. The third exercise shows how proper chaining is essential when using the morph spiral cutting method. The fourth exercise uses an entry point to start the pocket toolpath.

Exercise 1 – Facing the Stock with High Speed Loops

The Facing toolpath quickly cleans the stock from the top of a part and creates an even surface for future operations. Remember to use overlap distances of at least 50% to prevent leaving little scallops of material at the edges of the stock. The completed toolpath for this exercise should look like the following picture:

In this exercise, you will:
- ◆ **Use Job Setup**
- ◆ **Create a facing toolpath**

▶ *Enter stock boundaries and select the tool*

1. Open **facing1.mc8**.

2. Choose
   - ◆ **MAIN MENU**
   - ◆ **Toolpaths**
   - ◆ **Job Setup**

3. Enter the values shown on the dialog box.

Note: Stock boundaries can be used to determine the geometry for a facing toolpath. No geometry selections are needed other than the stock boundaries from Job Setup.

4. Choose **OK**.

5. Choose **Face**.

6. Save the NCI file as **facing1.nci**.

7. Choose **Done**.

8. Right-click in the tool display area and select the 1" flat endmill.

▶ **Enter the facing parameters**

1. Select the **Facing parameters** tab.

2. Enter the values shown on the following dialog box.

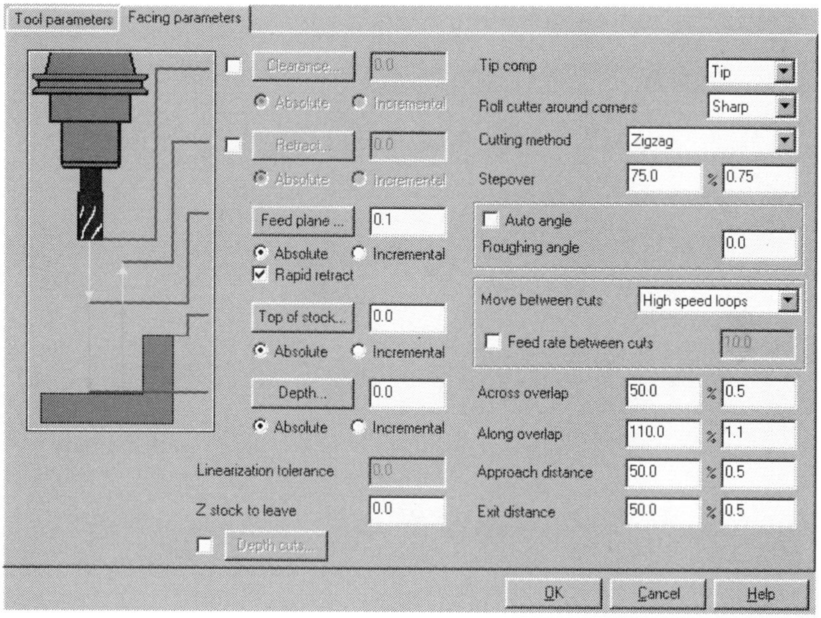

Note: The Move between cuts field is set to High speed loops to provide smooth movement between passes. This type of motion reduces wear and tear on the tool.

3. Choose **OK**.

The completed toolpath should look like the following picture:

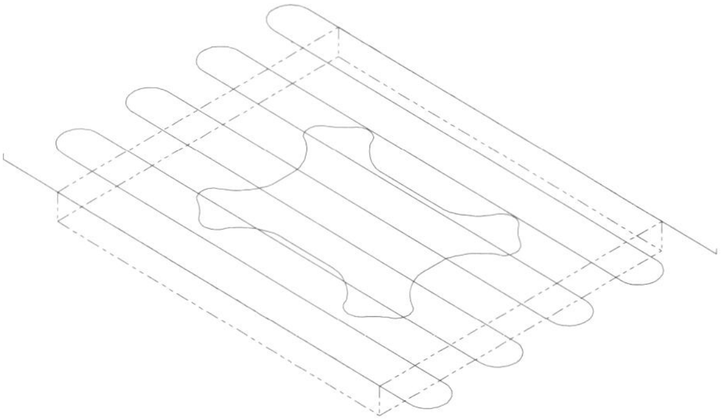

Exercise 2 – Using Different Pocket Cutting Methods

Seven cutting methods are available in the Mastercam pocketing function and each cutting method has advantages and disadvantages. The parallel spiral cutting method creates a relatively short NC program but does not guarantee complete cleanout depending on the shape of the pocket and the stepover of each pass. The constant overlap spiral cutting method analyzes stock after each pass and cleans out more stock than parallel spiral. The following pictures show the final pocket toolpath and the dimensions for the part used in this exercise.

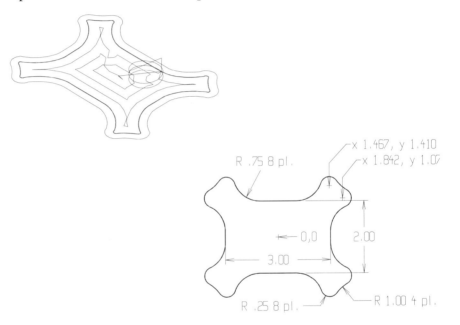

In this exercise, you will:

◆ **Use Toolpaths, Pocket**
◆ **Regenerate toolpaths in the Operations Manager**
◆ **Use the Parallel Spiral cutting method**
◆ **Use the Constant Overlap Spiral cutting method**
◆ **Use Helical entry**

▶ **Chain the pocket toolpath and select the tool**

1. Open **pocket1.mc8**.

2. Choose
   - ◆ **MAIN MENU**
   - ◆ **Toolpaths**
   - ◆ **Pocket**

3. Save the NCI file as **pocket1.nci**.

4. *Select chain 1.* Select the geometry as shown in the picture. Notice the chain direction is clockwise.

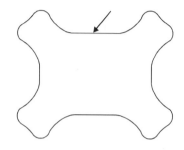

5. Choose **Done**.

6. Right-click in the tool display area.

7. Choose **Get tool from library**.

8. Select the 3/8" flat endmill and choose **OK**.

▶ **Enter the pocketing parameters**

1. Select the **Pocketing parameters** tab.

2. Enter the values shown on the following dialog box.

▶ Enter the roughing/finishing parameters

1. Select the **Roughing/Finishing parameters** tab.

2. Enter the values shown on the following dialog box.

3. Choose **OK**.

▶ *Backplot and verify the toolpath*

1. Choose **Operations**. The Operations Manager displays.

2. Choose the **Backplot** button.

3. On the Backplot menu, set the **Verify** option to **Y** (Yes).

Tip: The Verify option shows areas in the toolpath where material has been missed. It also marks the tool's position during the toolpath with a white circle.

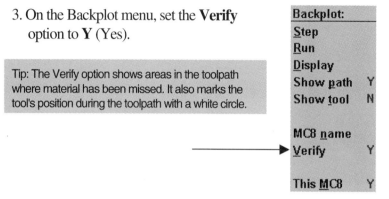

Backplot:
Step
Run
Display
Show path   Y
Show tool   N

MC8 name
→ Verify   Y

This MC8   Y

4. Choose **Run**. The entire backplot is completed at once. The toolpath should look like the following picture:

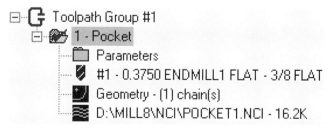

Tip: Notice the areas that were not cleaned out by the Parallel Spiral cutting method. (with a large overlap)

5. Choose **BACKUP** to return to the Operations Manager.

▶ *Change the cutting method*

1. Choose the **Parameters** icon for the toolpath.

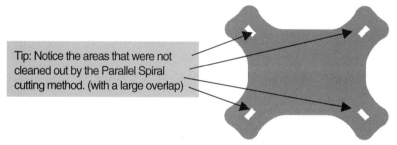

Toolpath Group #1
    1 - Pocket
        Parameters
        #1 - 0.3750 ENDMILL1 FLAT - 3/8 FLAT
        Geometry - (1) chain(s)
        D:\MILL8\NCI\POCKET1.NCI - 16.2K

2. Choose the **Roughing/Finishing parameters** tab.

Constant
Overlap Spiral

3. Select the **Constant Overlap Spiral** cutting method.

4. Choose the **Advanced** button on the Pocketing parameters tab.

5. Enter the values shown on the following dialog box.

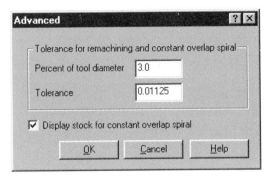

6. Choose **OK**.

▶ *Regenerate and display the toolpath*

1. Regenerate the modified toolpath.

2. Choose the **Backplot** button.

3. Choose **Run** to move through the toolpath. The toolpath should look like the following picture.

Note: Make sure the Verify option is set to Y (Yes).

Tip: The Constant Overlap Spiral cutting method cleaned out all of the stock by recalculating the amount of stock left after each roughing pass.

4. Choose **BACKUP** to return to the Operations Manager.

▶ *Add a helical entry and change the tolerance for the constant overlap spiral*

1. Choose the **Parameters** icon for the toolpath.

2. Choose the **Roughing/Finishing parameters** tab.

3. Select the **Entry – helix** check box and choose the **Entry - helix** button.

4. Enter the values shown on the following dialog box.

Helix/Ramp Parameters

Helix | Ramp

Minimum radius: 10.0 % 0.0375

Maximum radius: 100.0 % 0.375

Z clearance: 0.05

XY clearance: 0.1

Plunge angle: 3.0

☑ Output arc moves

Tolerance: 0.0

☑ Center on entry point

Direction
- ⦿ CW   ○ CCW

☑ Follow boundary
☑ On failure only
if length exceeds: 0.5

If all entry attempts fail
⦿ Plunge   ○ Skip
☐ Save skipped boundary

Entry rate
⦿ Plunge rate   ○ Feed rate

OK | Cancel | Help

Note: Z clearance is the distance above the top of stock where the helix starts.

5. Choose **OK** twice.

▶ *Regenerate the toolpath*

Regenerate the modified toolpath. The toolpath should look like the following picture:

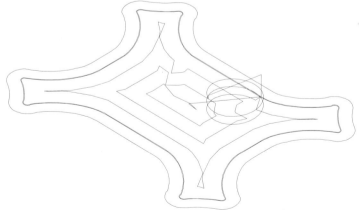

Exercise 3 – Using the Morph Spiral Cutting Method and the Chain Manager

The morph spiral cutting method roughs a pocket by gradually interpolating between the outer boundary and the island. It is important, however, to chain the outer boundary and the island correctly so that the chains are synchronized. If you chain the pocket incorrectly, you can fix the error using the Chain Manager dialog box. The morph spiral cutting method should only be used on parts with one island. The final toolpath should look like the following picture:

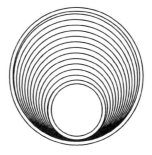

In this exercise, you will:

- ◆ **Use Toolpaths, Pocket**
- ◆ **Use the Morph Spiral cutting method**
- ◆ **Use the Chain Manager**

▶ *Chain the pocket toolpath and select the tool*

1. Open **pocket2.mc8**.

2. Choose
   - ◆ **MAIN MENU**
   - ◆ **Toolpaths**
   - ◆ **Pocket**

3. Save the NCI file as **pocket2.nci**.

4. Select the outer boundary at position 1.

5. Select the island at position 2.

6. Choose **Done**.

7. Right-click in the tool display area and select the 5/16" flat endmill.

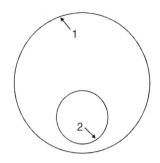

▶ *Enter the pocketing parameters*

1. Select the **Pocketing parameters** tab.

2. Enter the values shown on the following dialog box.

| Tool parameters | Pocketing parameters | Roughing/Finishing parameters |

☐ Clearance... `1.0`
  ○ Absolute   ○ Incremental

☐ Retract... `0.0`
  ○ Absolute   ○ Incremental

Feed plane... `0.1`
  ● Absolute   ○ Incremental
  ☑ Rapid retract

Top of stock... `0.0`
  ○ Absolute   ● Incremental

Depth... `0.0`
  ○ Absolute   ● Incremental

Machining direction
  ● Climb   ○ Conventional

Tip comp `Tip ▼`

Roll cutter around corners `Sharp ▼`

Linearization tolerance `0.001`

XY stock to leave `0.0`

Z stock to leave `0.0`

☐ Create additional finish operation

Pocket type: `Standard ▼`   ☐ Depth cuts...   ☐ Filter...

Facing...   Remachining...   Open pockets...   Advanced...

OK   Cancel   Help

▶ Enter the roughing/finishing parameters

1. Select the **Roughing/Finishing parameters** tab.

2. Enter the values shown on the following dialog box.

Tool parameters	Pocketing parameters	Roughing/Finishing parameters

☑ Rough   Cutting method: Morph Spiral

Zigzag	Constant Overlap Spiral	Parallel Spiral	Parallel Spiral, Clean Corners	Morph Spiral	True Spiral	One Way

Stepover percentage `75.0`   Roughing angle `0.0`   ☐ Spiral inside to outside

Stepover distance `0.23438`   ☐ Minimize tool burial   ☐ Entry - helix

☐ Finish

No. of passes `1`   Finish pass spacing `0.01`

☑ Finish outer boundary   Cutter compensation `computer`

☐ Start finish pass at closest entity   ☐ Optimize cutter comp in control

☐ Keep tool down   ☐ Machine finish passes only at final depth

☑ Machine finish passes after roughing all pockets   ☐ Lead in/out...

OK	Cancel	Help

3. Choose **OK**. The completed toolpath should look like the following picture:

Tip: This toolpath does not have the correct chain synchronization. The tool makes unnecessary moves around the island. If this toolpath was chained using different start points, the tool would have a more constant load and you would be able to use a higher feed rate to get the job done faster.

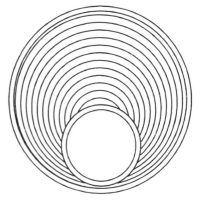

▶ *Change the start point of the chains*

1. Choose **Operations**. The Operations Manager displays.

2. Choose the **Geometry** icon for the toolpath.

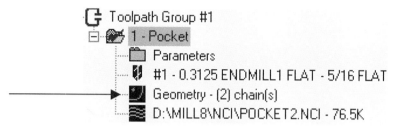

3. The Chain Manager dialog box opens. Right-click on **Chain 1**.

4. Choose **Start point** from the right-click menu.

5. Choose **Forward step** from the menu. The start point arrow moves to the opposite side of the circle.

6. Choose **Done**.

7. Choose **OK**.

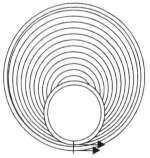

▶ *Regenerate the toolpath*

Regenerate the modified toolpath. The toolpath should look like the following picture:

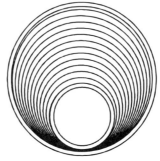

Exercise 4 - Specifying an Entry Point

Specifying an entry point for a pocket toolpath can be necessary for tools that cannot plunge directly into the material. You could drill a hole in the material at the entry point and start the pocket toolpath in that hole. If you chain a point when chaining a pocket toolpath, Mastercam automatically uses this point as the entry point for the toolpath. The final toolpath for this exercise should look like the following picture:

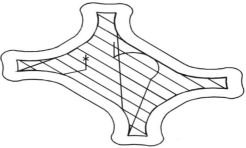

In this exercise you will:

◆ **Use Toolpaths, Pocket**
◆ **Use an entry point in a pocket toolpath**
◆ **Use Lead in/out on finish pass**

▶ *Chain the pocket toolpath and select the tool*

1. Open **pocket3.mc8**.

2. Choose
   - ◆ **MAIN MENU**
   - ◆ **Toolpaths**
   - ◆ **Pocket**

3. Save the NCI file as **pocket3.nci**.

4. *Select chain 1.* Select the point at position 1.

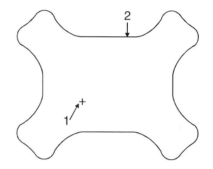

5. *Select chain 2.* Select the boundary at position 2.

6. Choose **Done**.

7. Right-click in the tool display area and select the 3/8" flat endmill.

Note: You could have selected either the point or the boundary first. Mastercam automatically knows that the point should be used as the entry point for the pocket toolpath.

▶ *Enter the pocketing parameters*

1. Select the **Pocketing parameters** tab.

2. Enter the values shown on the following dialog box.

▶ *Enter the roughing/finishing parameters*

1. Select the **Roughing/Finishing parameters** tab.

2. Enter the values shown on the following dialog box.

3. Choose the **Lead in/out** button.

4. Enter the values shown on the following dialog box.

Note: Adding a lead in/out to the finish pass prevents a dwell mark on the part at the end of the toolpath.

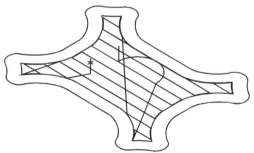

5. Choose **OK** twice. The completed toolpath should look like the following picture.

8 *Using Advanced Pocket and Contour Toolpaths*

This chapter covers more advanced methods of creating pocket and contour toolpaths. The first exercise focuses on using pocket remachining to clean out material quickly and efficiently. The second exercise combines pocket depth cuts, tapered walls, and island facing to remove material from a more complicated part with multiple islands. The third exercise demonstrates the subprogram feature with contour depth cuts. The fourth exercise demonstrates a contour ramp toolpath. The final exercise shows you how to modify a contour toolpath using the Toolpath Editor.

Exercise 1 – Remachining

Using remachining in pocket toolpaths can save time by getting in the part with a large tool and quickly cleaning out as much material as possible. You can then go back into the part with a smaller tool and clean out the areas that the large tool was not able to reach. The following pictures show the final rough and finish toolpaths for this exercise.

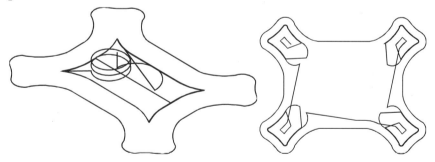

In this exercise, you will:
- ◆ **Use Toolpaths, Pocket**
- ◆ **Use Remachining**
- ◆ **Use the Rough entry and Lead in/out features**

▶ *Chain the pocket geometry and select the tool*

1. Open **pocket4.mc8**.

2. Choose
   - ◆ **MAIN MENU**
   - ◆ **Toolpaths**
   - ◆ **Pocket**

3. Save the NCI file as **pocket4.nci**.

4. *Select chain 1.* Select the boundary as shown in the picture at right.

5. Choose **Done**.

6. Right-click in the tool display area and select the 1" flat endmill.

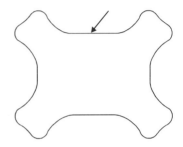

▶ *Enter the pocketing parameters*

1. Select the **Pocketing parameters** tab.

2. Enter the values shown on the following dialog box.

▶ *Enter the roughing/finishing parameters*

1. Select the **Roughing/Finishing parameters** tab.

2. Enter the values shown on the following dialog box.

3. Choose the **Entry – helix** button.

4. Enter the values shown on the following dialog box.

Tip: These options prevent the tool from plunging directly into the material by adding a helix or ramp to the start of the pocket toolpath.

5. Choose **OK**.

6. Choose the **Lead in/out** button.

7. Enter the values shown on the following dialog box.

Lead In/Out   `? X`

Overlap `0.125`

☑ Entry   ☑ Exit

┌─ Line ──────────────────────┐   ┌─ Line ──────────────────────┐
│ ○ Perpendicular ⦿ Tangent │   │ ○ Perpendicular ⦿ Tangent │
│ Length: `0.0`   % `0.0`   │   │ Length: `0.0`   % `0.0`   │
│ Ramp height: `0.0`   │   │ Ramp height: `0.0`   │
└─────────────────────────────┘   └─────────────────────────────┘

┌─ Arc ───────────────────────┐ → ┌─ Arc ───────────────────────┐
│ Radius: `50.0` % `0.5`   │   │ Radius: `50.0` % `0.5`   │
│ Sweep: `90.0`   │   │ Sweep: `90.0`   │
│ Helix height: `0.0`   │   │ Helix height: `0.0`   │
└─────────────────────────────┘   └─────────────────────────────┘

☐ Use entry point   ☐ Use exit point
☐ Use point depth   ☐ Use point depth
☐ Enter on first depth cut only   ☐ Exit on last depth cut only

              `OK`   `Cancel`   `Help`

Note: The lead in/out parameters allow the tool to enter the part tangentially.

8. Choose **OK** twice. The toolpath should look like the following picture:

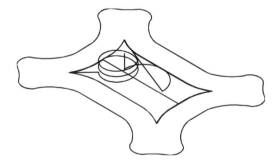

▶ *Chain the remachining geometry and select the tool*

1. Choose **Pocket**.

2. *Select chain 1.* Select the same boundary as the first pocket toolpath.

3. Choose **Done**.

4. Right-click in the tool display area and select the 3/8" flat endmill.

▶ *Enter the pocketing parameters*

1. Select the **Pocketing parameters** tab.

2. Enter the values shown on the following dialog box.

3. Choose the **Remachining** button.

4. Enter the values shown on the following dialog box.

5. Choose **OK**.

▶ *Enter the roughing/finishing parameters*

1. Select the **Roughing/Finishing parameters** tab.

2. Enter the values shown on the following dialog box.

3. Choose the **Lead in/out** button.

4. Enter the values shown on the following dialog box.

Lead In/Out

Overlap   0.125

☑ Entry

Line
○ Perpendicular ● Tangent

Length: 0.0   %   0.0

Ramp height: 0.0

Arc
Radius: 66.66667   %   0.25

Sweep: 90.0

Helix height: 0.0

☐ Use entry point
☐ Use point depth
☐ Enter on first depth cut only

☑ Exit

Line
○ Perpendicular ● Tangent

Length: 0.0   %   0.0

Ramp height: 0.0

Arc
Radius: 66.66667   %   0.25

Sweep: 90.0

Helix height: 0.0

☐ Use exit point
☐ Use point depth
☐ Exit on last depth cut only

OK   Cancel   Help

5. Choose **OK** twice.

6. *Machinable area for rough tool.* The area in red shows the material that the rough tool was able to remove. Press [Enter] to continue.

7. *Machinable area for finish tool.* The area in yellow shows the material that the finish tool was able to remove. Press [Enter] to continue.

8. *Remaining stock.* The area in yellow shows the stock that remains for the finish tool to remove. This area is shown on the following picture. Press [Enter] to continue.

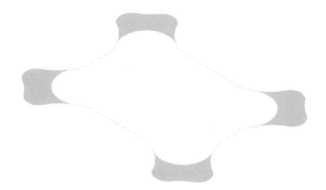

9. *Remaining stock after remachining. Area = 0.0000* Press [Enter] to continue. The remachining toolpath should look like the following picture.

Note: The Area should equal zero (0) in this example. If it does not equal zero, try reducing the stepover percentage on the Roughing/finishing parameters dialog box. Another reason the area might not equal zero is that the cutter radius is karger than the arc radius in the part.

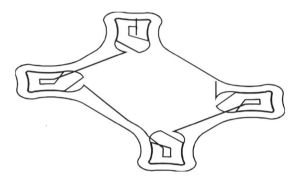

Exercise 2 – Using Depth Cuts, Island Facing, and Tapered Walls

Depth cuts, island facing, and tapered walls are often used together on more complex pocket toolpaths. For example, tapered walls require multiple depth cuts so that the offset for the walls can be computed at each depth. Also, when you face the islands, Mastercam automatically uses the island depth as one of the depth cut values. The completed toolpath should look like the following picture:

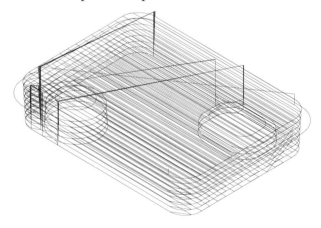

In this exercise, you will:

◆ **Use Toolpaths, Pocket**
◆ **Change to a metric tool library**
◆ **Use Depth cuts**
◆ **Use Island facing**
◆ **Use Tapered walls**

▶ *Chain the pocket geometry*

1. Open **pocket5.mc8**.

2. Choose

◆ **MAIN MENU**
◆ **Toolpaths**
◆ **Pocket**

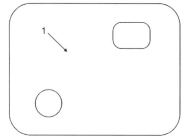

3. Save the NCI file as **pocket5.nci**.

4. Choose **Area**.

5. Select position 1.

6. Choose **Done**.

▶ *Select a metric tool*

1. Right-click in the tool display area.

2. Choose **Get tool from library**.

3. Right-click in the tool library window.

4. Choose **Change library** from the right-click menu.

5. Select **tools_mm.tl8** and choose **Save**.

6. Select a 15 mm flat endmill and choose **OK**.

▶ *Enter the pocketing parameters*

1. Select the **Pocketing parameters** tab.

2. Enter the values shown on the following dialog box.

3. Choose the **Depth cuts** button.

4. Enter the values shown on the following dialog box.

Tip: The toolpath may use a smaller step size than the Max rough step because Mastercam calculates equal steps less than or equal to the max rough step between the top of stock and the final depth.

Tip: This value sets the taper for the outer boundary.

5. Choose **OK**.

6. Choose the **Facing** button.

7. Enter the values shown on the following dialog box.

Tip: Island facing trims islands to the correct height, instead of using one of the depth cuts to clean off the top of the islands. Therefore, you do not have to create a depth cut at the height of each island.

Facing

Overlap percentage:	50.0
Overlap amount:	7.5
Approach distance:	0.0
Exit distance:	0.0
Stock above islands:	0.0

OK   Cancel   Help

8. Choose **OK**.

▶ *Enter the roughing/finishing parameters*

1. Select the **Roughing/Finishing parameters** tab.

2. Enter the values shown on the following dialog box.

Tool parameters | Pocketing parameters | Roughing/Finishing parameters

☑ Rough   Cutting method: Zigzag

Zigzag   Constant Overlap Spiral   Parallel Spiral   Parallel Spiral, Clean Corners   Morph Spiral   True Spiral   One Way

Stepover percentage	60.0
Stepover distance	9.0

Roughing angle 0.0
☐ Minimize tool burial

☐ Spiral inside to outside
☐ Entry - helix

☑ Finish

No. of passes 1   Finish pass spacing 0.5

☑ Finish outer boundary   Cutter compensation computer ▼

☐ Start finish pass at closest entity   ☐ Optimize cutter comp in control

☐ Keep tool down   ☐ Machine finish passes only at final depth

☑ Machine finish passes after roughing all pockets   ☑ Lead in/out...

OK   Cancel   Help

3. Choose the **Lead in/out** button.

4. Enter the values shown on the following dialog box.

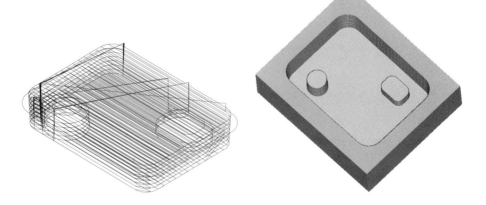

Note: Using entry and exit arcs prevents the toolpath from plunging directly into the pocket and leaving a dwell mark.

5. Choose **OK** twice. The completed toolpath should look like the following pictures. Note the steps on the outer boundary of the pocket and the pocket islands that show the taper angles.

Exercise 3 – Using Subprograms

The part in this exercise uses contour depth cuts, to demonstrate using subprograms. A subprogram is a section of an NCI file that repeats at different locations, thereby reducing the file's size. This exercise shows you the effect on the NC code by using a subprogram. Subprograms can also be used on pocket depth cuts, circle mill toolpaths, drill toolpaths, and transform toolpaths.

In this exercise, you will:
- ◆ **Use Toolpaths, Contour, Depth cuts, Subprogram**
- ◆ **View the resulting NC file**

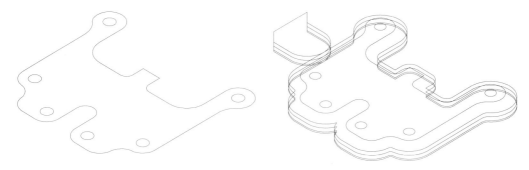

▶ *Open the file and generate the toolpath*

1. Open **subprogram.mc8**.

2. Choose
   - ◆ **MAIN MENU**
   - ◆ **Toolpaths**
   - ◆ **Contour**

3. Save the NCI file as **subprogram.nci**.

4. Chain the contour at position 1 as shown in the following figure. Make sure the arrow points in the clockwise direction. If it does not, choose **Reverse**.

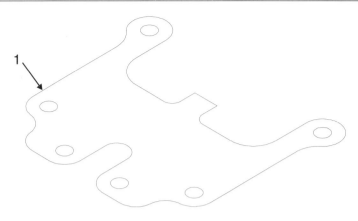

5. Choose **Done**.

6. If you are still using the **tools_mm.tl8** tool library, change the tool library back to the default of **tools.tl8**.

7. Select the ¾" flat endmill.

8. Select the **Contour parameters** tab.

9. Enter the values shown on the following dialog box.

10. Choose the **Depth cuts** button.

11. Enter the values shown on the following dialog box.

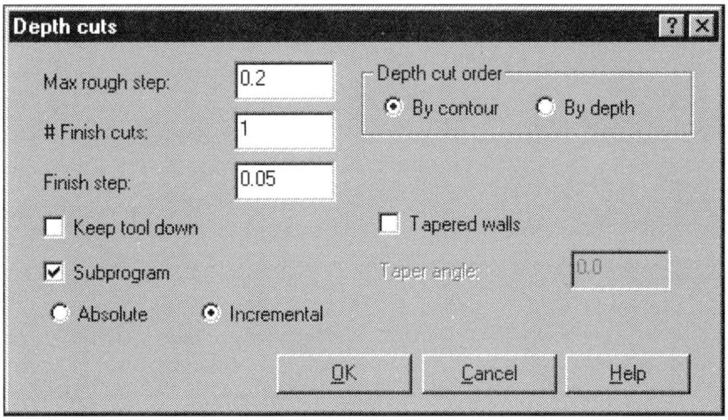

12. Choose **OK**.

13. Choose the **Lead in/out** button.

14. Enter the values shown on the following dialog box.

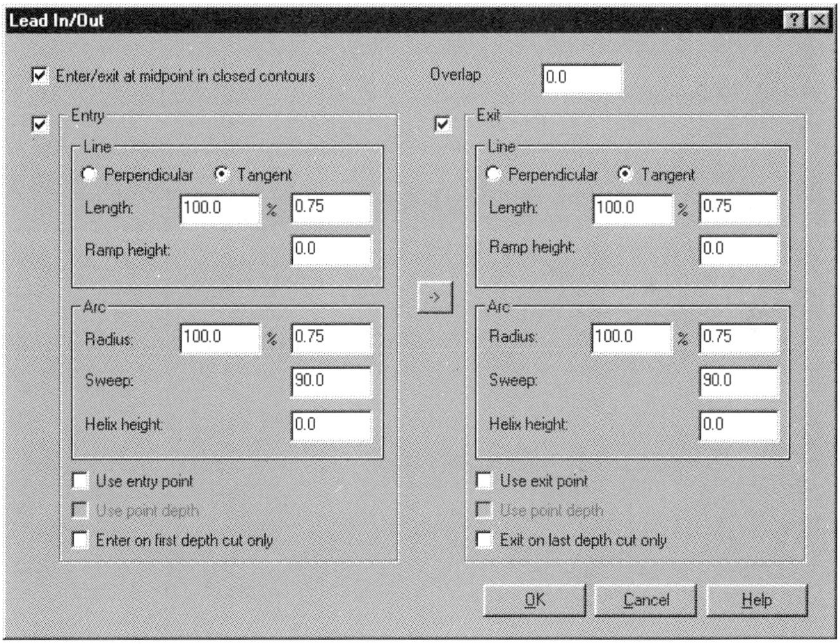

15. Choose **OK** twice. Mastercam generates the toolpath as shown in the following picture.

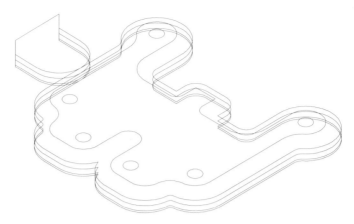

▶ *Post the operation and view the NC file*

1. Choose
   - ◆ **MAIN MENU**
   - ◆ **Toolpaths**
   - ◆ **Operations**

2. Choose **Post**.

3. Enter the values shown on the following dialog box.

4. Choose **OK**.

5. Choose **Save** to save the NCI file as **subprogram.nci**, and choose **Save** to save the NC file as **subprogram.nc**. Mastercam displays the NC file in the default text editor. The NC file should look like the following picture.

```
%
O0000
(PROGRAM NAME - SUBPROGRAM CR)
(DATE=DD-MM-YY - 21-01-00 TIME=HH:MM - 12:34)
(3/4 TOOL - 3 DIA. OFF. - 43 LEN. - 3 DIA. - .75)
N100G20
N102G0G40G49G80G90
N104T3M6
N106G0G90G54X-3.7229Y-.4937S713M3
N108G43H3Z.25
N110G1Z-.15F6.42
N112X-3.4729
N114G3X-2.9729Y.0063R.5
N116M98P1001
N186G3X-3.4729Y.5063R.5
N188G1X-3.7229
N190G0Z.25
N192Y-.4937
N194G1Z-.3
N196X-3.4729
N198G3X-2.9729Y.0063R.5
N200M98P1001
N270G3X-3.4729Y.5063R.5
N272G1X-3.7229
N274G0Z.25
N276Y-.4937
N278G1Z-.45
```

Tip: The M98 or M99 code is a subprogram indicator.

The subprogram indicator is used instead of repeated lines of code, reducing the size of the NC file.

6. Close the text editor.

7. Choose **OK** to close the Operations Manager.

Exercise 4 – Using Contour Ramp

In this exercise, the contour toolpath includes a ramping motion to move between depth cuts. The ramp uses constant stepdown in the Z axis which can be effective for high-speed machining. The following picture shows the completed toolpath.

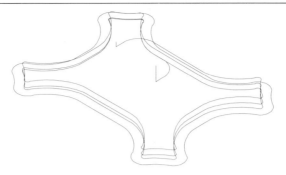

In this exercise, you will:

- ◆ **Use Toolpaths, Contour**
- ◆ **Use the Contour ramp feature**
- ◆ **Use Lead in/out**

▶ *Chain the geometry and select the tool*

1. Open **rampctr.mc8**.

2. Choose
   - ◆ **MAIN MENU**
   - ◆ **Toolpaths**
   - ◆ **Contour**

3. Save the NCI file as **rampctr.nci**.

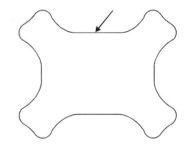

4. *Select chain 1.* Select the boundary as shown in the picture at right. Make sure the chaining direction is clockwise.

5. Choose **Done**.

6. Right-click in the tool display area and select the 3/8" flat endmill.

▶ *Enter the contour parameters and generate the toolpath*

1. Select the **Contour parameters** tab.

2. Enter the values shown on the following dialog box.

3. Choose the **Ramp** button and enter the values shown on the following dialog box.

4. Choose **OK**.

5. Choose the **Lead in/out** button and enter the values shown on the following dialog box.

Lead In/Out

☐ Enter/exit at midpoint in closed contours   Overlap   [0.25]

☑ ┌Entry─────────────────────────────┐
  │ ┌Line──────────────────────────┐ │
  │ │ ○ Perpendicular ⦿ Tangent   │ │
  │ │ Length: [50.0] % [0.1875] │ │
  │ │ Ramp height: [0.0]   │ │
  │ └──────────────────────────────┘ │
  │ ┌Arc───────────────────────────┐ │
  │ │ Radius: [100.0] % [0.375] │ │
  │ │ Sweep: [90.0]   │ │
  │ │ Helix height: [0.0]   │ │
  │ └──────────────────────────────┘ │
  │ ☐ Use entry point   │
  │ ☐ Use point depth   │
  │ ☐ Enter on first depth cut only │
  └──────────────────────────────────┘

☑ ┌Exit──────────────────────────────┐
  │ ┌Line──────────────────────────┐ │
  │ │ ○ Perpendicular ⦿ Tangent   │ │
  │ │ Length: [50.0] % [0.1875] │ │
  │ │ Ramp height: [0.0]   │ │
  │ └──────────────────────────────┘ │
  │ ┌Arc───────────────────────────┐ │
  │ │ Radius: [100.0] % [0.375] │ │
  │ │ Sweep: [90.0]   │ │
  │ │ Helix height: [0.0]   │ │
  │ └──────────────────────────────┘ │
  │ ☐ Use exit point   │
  │ ☐ Use point depth   │
  │ ☐ Exit on last depth cut only   │
  └──────────────────────────────────┘

[OK]   [Cancel]   [Help]

6. Choose **OK** twice. Mastercam generates the toolpath.

7. Choose **Operations** to open the Operations Manager.

8. Choose **Backplot** and step through the backplot to see the results of contour ramp. The toolpath should look like the following picture.

Note: There are no direct steps in between successive depths. The cutter is constantly moving in the negative Z direction.

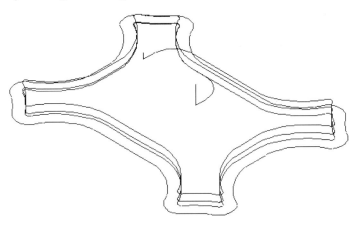

Exercise 5 – Modifying a Toolpath Using the Toolpath Editor

This exercise shows you how to make corrections to a toolpath using Mastercam's graphical Toolpath Editor. The Toolpath Editor gives you a fine level of control over the motion in your toolpaths. You can make modifications to the tool motion created by Mastercam and change the areas of the part that are machined. These changes are not associative. After you make changes using the Toolpath Editor, the NCI file for the operation is locked so you do not overwrite the changes you have made by regenerating the toolpath. The following picture shows the geometry and original toolpath for this exercise.

In this exercise, you will:

◆ **Modify tool motion on selected points using the Toolpath Editor**

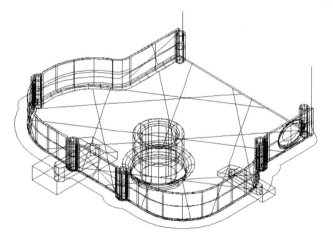

▶ *Modify the toolpath using the Toolpath Editor*

1. Open **tp_editor.mc8**.

2. Choose
    ◆ **MAIN MENU**
    ◆ **Toolpaths**
    ◆ **Operations**
    ◆ **Backplot**
    ◆ **Step**

3. When the backplot is complete, choose **OK** and choose **BACKUP**.

Note: The original toolpath would crash into the clamps on the part. You can use the Toolpath Editor to adjust the toolpath to avoid the clamps.

4. In the Operations Manager, right-click on the **NCI** icon for the operation. The Toolpath Editor opens.

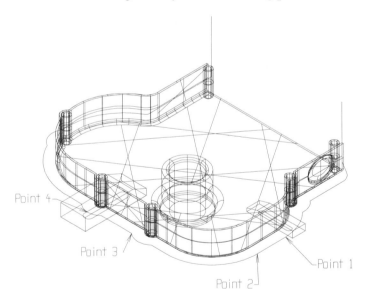

Note: You can move the dialog box to the top of the graphics window to view the toolpath while you make edits.

5. Use the up arrow scroll key in the **Point** edit box to move to point 10. This is Point 1 shown on the geometry in the following picture.

6. Choose the **Options** button.

7. Under Point Insertion Mode, choose the **After** option and choose **OK**.

8. Choose the **Edit** button. This method insert points in order to avoid the clamps.

9. Choose
   - ◆ **Add Point**
   - ◆ **Relative**
   - ◆ **Last**
   - ◆ **Rectang**

10. Type **z2** in the prompt area and press [Enter].

11. Choose the **Select** button and select Point 2 on the geometry as shown in the picture above.

12. Choose the **Options** button. Under Point Insertion Mode, choose the **Before** option and choose **OK**.

13. Choose the **Edit** button.

14. Choose
   - ◆ **Add Point**
   - ◆ **Relative**
   - ◆ **Last**
   - ◆ **Rectang**

15. Type **z2** in the prompt area and press [Enter].

16. Choose
   - ◆ **Edit**
   - ◆ **Edit Point**

17. When the Edit Point Parameters dialog opens, choose **Rapid Move**. This turns the tool motion into a rapid move. Choose **OK**.

18. Use the up arrow scroll key in the **Point** edit box to move to point 11. This is the first point that you added.

19. Choose
   - ◆ **Edit**
   - ◆ **Edit Point**

20. When the Edit Point Parameters dialog opens, choose **Rapid Move**. This turns the tool motion into a rapid move. Choose **OK**.

21. Another method to avoid the clamps is to delete a section of the toolpath. Choose the **Select** button and select point 3 on the geometry as shown in the following picture.

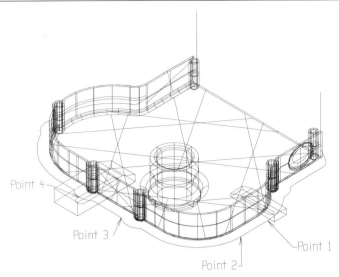

22. Choose the **Edit** button and choose
    - ◆ **Del Section**
    - ◆ **Forward Step**
    - ◆ **Done**
    - ◆ **OK**

23. Choose the **Select** button and select point 4 on the geometry as shown in the above picture and choose
    - ◆ **Edit**
    - ◆ **Edit Point**

24. Turn on the **Rapid Move** option, set the Rapid Height to **2.0**, and choose **OK**.

25. Choose **OK** to close the Toolpath Editor. The Operations Manager opens.

```
⊟ ● Toolpath Group #1
   ⊟ 📂 1 - Contour (2D) - Level #1
      📄 Parameters
      📎 #1 - 0.7500 ENDMILL3 BULL - 3/4 BULL ENDMILL 0.062
      📄 Geometry - (1) chain(s)
   ──────────────▶ 📄 C:\MILL8\NCI\OPEN POCKET.NCI - 3.4K
```

The Operations Manager shows a red lock over the NCI icon for the toolpath and the operation group icon that contains the locked toolpath. The toolpath is automatically locked because you used the Toolpath Editor.

9 Importing, Grouping, and Saving Operations

This chapter shows you how to create drill and pocket toolpaths and use the Import/Save functions to apply these operations to similar parts. In Exercise 1, you create a part. In Exercise 2, you apply drill and pocket toolpaths to the part and save the drill toolpath parameters to a library. In Exercise 3, you import the drill and pocket parameters created in Exercise 2 and apply them to a similar part. This chapter also shows you how to use both geometry groups and operation groups to organize and streamline your work.

Exercise 1 – Designing the Part

Open the file **cover.mc8** that you created in Chapter 1. Use the techniques you learned in previous chapters to finish the part, as shown in the following picture.

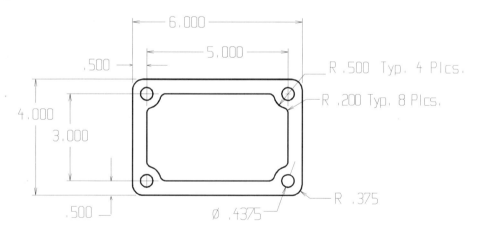

Exercise 2 – Creating Drill and Pocket Operations

In this exercise, using the part you created in Exercise 1, you create a geometry group that can be selected for many Mastercam functions, such as toolpaths. You then create drill and pocket toolpaths for the part. Once you create the operations, you save them to a library.

In this exercise, you will:

- ◆ **Use geometry groups**
- ◆ **Create drill and pocket toolpaths**
- ◆ **Add drill points**
- ◆ **Use the Drill/Counterbore parameters**
- ◆ **Copy operations**
- ◆ **Save operations to a library**

▶ *Open the file, create a geometry group, and begin the drill toolpath*

1. Open **cover.mc8**.

2. Choose **Groups** from the Secondary Menu.

3. Choose **New**.

4. *Enter unique group name.* Type in **Drill Holes** in the prompt area and press [Enter].

5. *Select entities to add to the group(s).* Select the four drill holes.

6. Choose **Done**.

7. Choose **OK**.

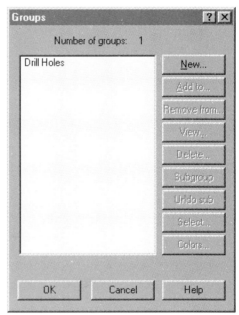

8. Choose
   - ◆ **MAIN MENU**
   - ◆ **Toolpaths**
   - ◆ **Drill**

9. Save the NCI file as **cover.nci**.

▶ *Add the drill points*

1. Choose **Entities**.

   Note: Choosing Entities places the drill points at the center of closed circles in the order that the circles were created.

2. Choose
   - ◆ **Group**
   - ◆ **Drill Holes**
   - ◆ **OK**

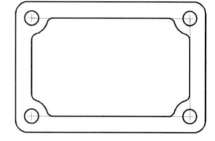

3. Choose **Done**. The drilling order displays as shown in the picture at right.

4. Choose **Done**.

▶ *Enter the tool and drill parameters*

1. Access the tool library and select a ¼" center drill.

2. Select the **Simple drill – no peck** tab.

3. Enter the values shown on the following dialog box.

Tool parameters	Simple drill - no peck	Custom Drill Parameters 1

Clearance... `1.0`

○ Absolute ○ Incremental

Cycle

`Drill/Counterbore` ▾

Retract... `0.1`

◉ Absolute ○ Incremental

1st peck `0.25`

Subsequent peck `0.25`

Top of stock... `0.0`

○ Absolute ◉ Incremental

Peck `0.04`

Chip break `0.04`

Depth... `0.0`

○ Absolute ◉ Incremental

Dwell `0.0`

Shift `0.0`

☑ Tip comp...

| OK | Cancel | Help |

4. Choose **OK.** The drill path displays as shown in the following picture.

Note: Selecting the Incremental option for the Top of stock and Depth parameters places these values relative to the chained geometry. This ensures that when you apply this operation to a different part, the depth of the drilled holes is incremental from the selected geometry.

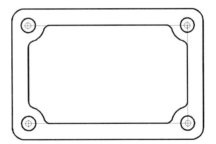

Identify the operation group

1. Choose **Operations**.

2. Right-click anywhere in the operations list area, and from the right-click menu, choose:
   - ◆ **Groups**
   - ◆ **Rename operation group**

3. Overwrite the operation group name with the name **Drill Operations** and press [Enter].

▶ *Copy the center drill operation and add drill and tap operations*

1. Right-click on the **Simple drill – no peck** operation.

2. Choose **Copy**.

3. Move the cursor below the first operation. Right-click and choose **Paste**.

4. Repeat the first 3 steps to paste the operation below operation 2 as shown in the picture to the right.

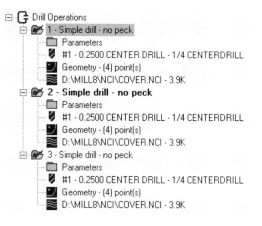

5. Choose the **Parameters** icon for operation 2.

6. Access the tool library and select a 25/64" drill.

7. Select the **Simple drill –no peck** tab.

8. Enter the values shown on the following dialog box.

9. Choose **OK**.

Note: Selecting the Peck drill cycle changes the Simple drill – no peck tab to say Peck drill – full retract.

10. Choose the **Parameters** icon for operation 3.

11. Access the tool library and select a 7/16 -20 right-hand tap.

12. Select the **Simple drill –no peck** tab.

13. Enter the values shown on the following dialog box.

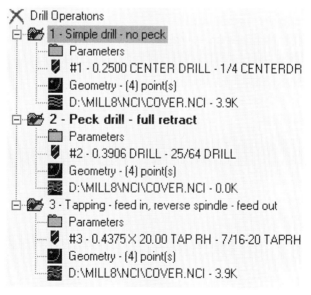

Note: Selecting the Tap drill cycle changes the Simple drill – no peck tab to say Tapping – feed in, reverse spindle – feed out tab.

14. Choose **OK**. The Operations Manager displays the three operations you created.

✕ Drill Operations
```
⊟ 1 - Simple drill - no peck
      Parameters
      #1 - 0.2500 CENTER DRILL - 1/4 CENTERDR
      Geometry - (4) point(s)
      D:\MILL8\NCI\COVER.NCI - 3.9K
⊟ 2 - Peck drill - full retract
      Parameters
      #2 - 0.3906 DRILL - 25/64 DRILL
      Geometry - (4) point(s)
      D:\MILL8\NCI\COVER.NCI - 0.0K
⊟ 3 - Tapping - feed in, reverse spindle - feed out
      Parameters
      #3 - 0.4375 X 20.00 TAP RH - 7/16-20 TAPRH
      Geometry - (4) point(s)
      D:\MILL8\NCI\COVER.NCI - 3.9K
```

15. Choose
   ◆ **Select All**
   ◆ **Regen Path**

◆ **OK**
◆ **Backplot**
◆ **Step**

16. Step through the three operations to view the toolpaths.

17. When the backplot is complete, choose **OK** to return to the Operations Manager

▶ *Save the drill operations group to a library*

1. Make sure all three operations are selected.

2. Right-click in the operations list area.

3. Choose **Save to library** from the right-click menu.

4. Name the library group **DrillOps**, as shown in the picture to the right.

Note: A library group name allows you to group toolpath groups. You can place operations from several different toolpath groups in a library group.

5. Choose **OK**. The three operations are now saved to the library.

Note: If you are prompted to save the operations using tools that already exist in the library, choose No.

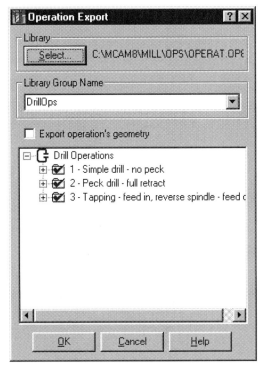

▶ *Chain the toolpath*

1. Right-click in the operation list are and choose
   - ◆ **Toolpaths**
   - ◆ **Pocket**

2. Select at position 1 to start the chain.

3. Choose **Done**.

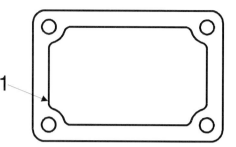

▶ *Select the tool and enter the toolpath parameters*

1. Access the tool library and select a 3/8" flat endmill.

2. Select the **Pocketing parameters** tab.

3. Enter the values shown on the following dialog box.

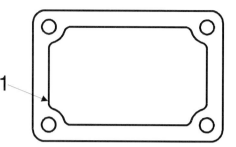

4. Select the **Roughing/Finishing parameters** tab.

5. Enter the values shown on the following dialog box.

Tool parameters	Pocketing parameters	Roughing/Finishing parameters

☑ Rough   Cutting method: Constant Overlap Spiral

Zigzag   **Constant Overlap Spiral**   Parallel Spiral   Parallel Spiral, Clean Corners   Morph Spiral   True Spiral   One Way

Stepover percentage `75.0`   Roughing angle `0.0`   ☐ Spiral inside to outside

Stepover distance `0.28125`   ☐ Minimize tool burial   ☑ Entry - helix

☑ Finish

No. of passes `1`   Finish pass spacing `0.01`

☑ Finish outer boundary   Cutter compensation `computer` ▼

☐ Start finish pass at closest entity   ☐ Optimize cutter comp in control

☐ Keep tool down   ☐ Machine finish passes only at final depth

☑ Machine finish passes after roughing all pockets   ☐ Lead in/out...

[OK]   [Cancel]   [Help]

6. Choose **OK**. Your toolpath should look like the following picture.

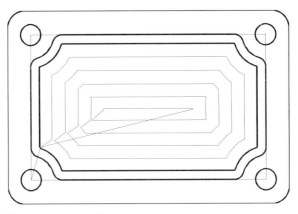

7. Save the file as **cover.mc8**.

Note: You have to save the file with the same name because when you import your toolpaths in the next exercise, the system searches for the file with the same name.

Exercise 3 - Import/Save Operations

The part used in this exercise requires drilled holes and pockets similar to the ones you created in Exercise 2. The following picture shows the dimensions of the part used in this exercise. This exercise shows you how to apply the drill and pocket toolpath parameters from Exercise 2 to a different part. You will:

- **Create drill and contour toolpaths**
- **Add drill points**
- **Import operations**

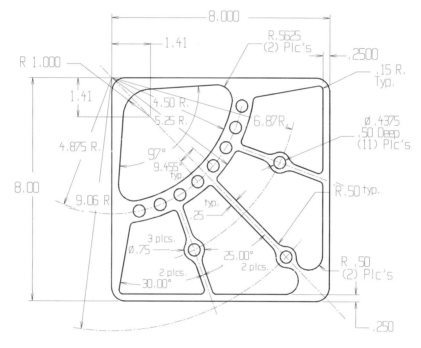

▶ *Open the file*

1. Open **imptsave.mc8**.

2. Save the file as **imptsave1.mc8**.

3. Choose
   - **MAIN MENU**
   - **Toolpaths**
   - **Drill**

4. Save the NCI file as **imptsave1.nci**.

▶ *Add the drill points*

1. Add the drill points to the
   .4375 holes by choosing
   Entities and selecting the
   holes individually or
   creating a geometry group.
   See Exercise 2 for more
   information.

2. Choose **Done**. Your drill
   path should look like the
   picture at right.

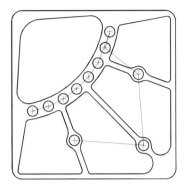

▶ *Import the drill operations*

1. Choose
   ◆ **Edit**
   ◆ **Import ops**

2. Select the **DrillOps** group
   that you saved in Exercise 2,
   as shown at right.

3. Choose **OK**. The completed
   drill toolpath is shown in the
   following picture.

*Note: If you are prompted to
add a tool that already exists,
choose Yes.*

Operation Import

Library
Select...   D:\MILL8\PRM\OPERAT.OP8

☐ Calculate speeds and feeds
☐ Assign current system tool and construction planes
☐ Import operation's geometry

DRILLOPS
⊞ 📁 1 - Simple drill - no peck
⊞ 📁 2 - Peck drill - full retract
⊞ 📁 3 - Tapping - feed in, reverse spindle - feed out

OK   Cancel   Help

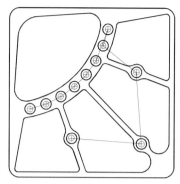

▶ *Import the pocket operation*

Note: In this procedure, you import the pocket toolpath parameters you created in Exercise 2.

1. Press [ALT + O] to open the Operations Manager.

2. Right-click in the operations list area.

3. Choose **Get from library** from the right-click menu. The Operation Import dialog box displays.

4. Choose **Select**. The Specify File Name to Read dialog box opens.

5. Locate the directory where you save your parts and choose **cover.mc8**.

6. Choose **Open**.

7. Select the Pocket folder as shown in the picture to the right.

8. Choose **OK**.

Note: If you are prompted to import the operation using a tool that already exists in the list, choose Yes.

The Operations Manager shows the three Drill operations and the Pocket operation that you imported.

Note: The Geometry icon for Operation 4 shows zero (0) chains. The pocket operation has been imported into the Operations Manager with no associated geometry. To complete the pocket operation, you must chain the geometry.

▶ *Chain the toolpath*

1. Choose the **Geometry** icon for Operation 4.

2. Right-click in the Chain Manager dialog box. The right-click menu displays.

3. Choose
   - ◆ **Add chain**
   - ◆ **Chain**
   - ◆ **Options**

The Chaining Options dialog box displays as shown in the following picture.

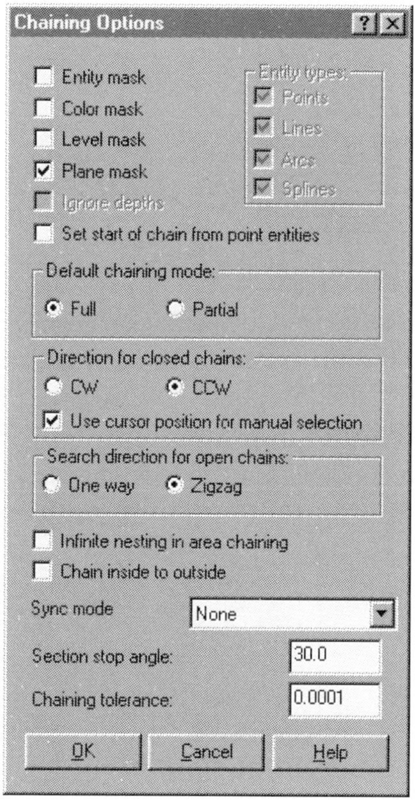

4. Select the **Plane mask** check box.

5. Choose **OK**.

Note: Change the Gview to Isometric to view the pocket depths.

6. Select at positions 1, 2, 3, 4,
   and 5 to chain the five
   pockets at the bottom of the
   part.

7. Choose **Done**. The Chain
   Manager displays the 5
   chains, as shown in the
   following picture.

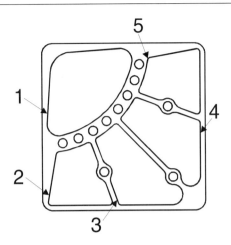

8. Choose
   ◆ **OK**
   ◆ **Select All**
   ◆ **Regen Path**

The completed toolpath should look like the following picture.

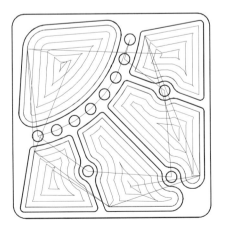

10 *Creating Circle Toolpaths*

Mastercam includes three circle toolpaths: circle mill, thread mill and automatic arc drill. Exercises 1 and 2 demonstrate a circle mill toolpath to machine a part with large, full circles for which drilling would not be efficient. In Exercise 3, a thread mill toolpath creates a series of helixes for effiectively machining a thread. The thread can be for either an inside or outside diameter. Exercise 4 shows how to use an automatic drill toolpath, which automatically selects a tool and other settings and is especially useful for parts with variously sized drill holes in multiple tool planes.

Exercise 1 –Creating a Circle Mill Toolpath

A circle mill toolpath can clean out arcs of different diameters in a single operation, as this exercise demonstrates. The geometry and toolpath are shown in the following picture:

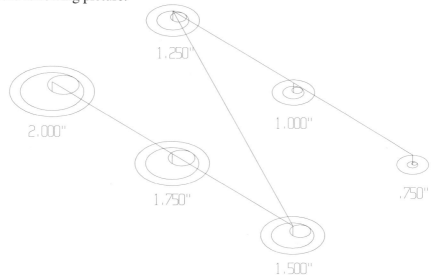

This exercise shows you how to create a circle mill toolpath. You will:

◆ **Use Toolpaths, Next Menu, Circ tlpths, Circle mill**

▶ *Create the circle mill toolpath*

1. Open **circmill.mc8**.

2. Choose
   - ◆ **MAIN MENU**
   - ◆ **Toolpaths**
   - ◆ **Next menu**
   - ◆ **Circ tlpths**
   - ◆ **Circle mill**

3. Save the NCI file as **circmill.nci**.

4. Choose
   - ◆ **Entities**
   - ◆ **All**
   - ◆ **Arcs**
   - ◆ **Done**
   - ◆ **Done**

5. Right-click in the tool display area and select the 1/2 inch flat endmill.

6. Select the **Circmill parameters** tab.

7. Enter the values shown on the following dialog box.

8. Choose **OK**. Mastercam generates the following toolpath.

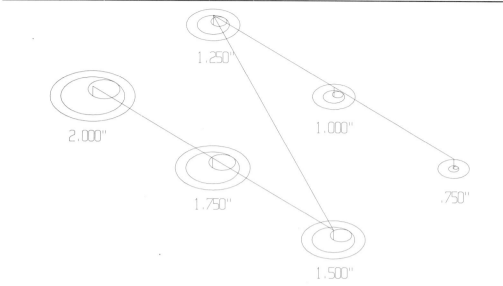

Exercise 2 –Adding Circle Mill Roughing

The circle mill toolpath does not remove enough material on the larger circles in the part above. To fix this, you can add roughing parameters, as this exercise demonstrates. The geometry and toolpath are shown in the following picture:

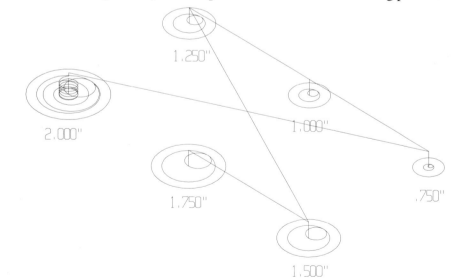

▶ *Create a circle mill operation for the 2-inch circle*

1. In the Operations Manager, make a copy of the circle mill operation by right-clicking on the operation, dragging the operation down, and selecting **Copy after**.

2. Change the geometry in the first operation by deleting the selected point for the 2-inch circle. In the Operations Manager, choose
   - ◆ **Geometry**
   - ◆ **Delete pts**

3. Select the center point of the 2-inch circle, and choose
   - ◆ **Backup**
   - ◆ **Done**

4. Change the geometry in the second operation by deleting the center point of all selected circles except the 2-inch circle. The Operations Manager should look like the following picture.

Delete the 2-inch circle in operation 1 so that 5 points are selected. ⟶

Delete all circles except the 2-inch circle in operation 2. ⟶

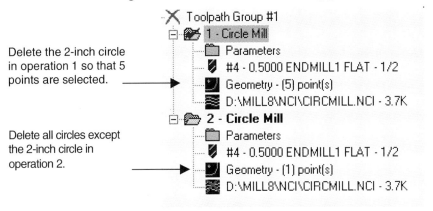

▶ *Select the roughing parameter and generate the toolpath*

1. Select **Parameters** icon for operation 2.

2. On the **Circmill Parameters** tab, select the **Roughing** button.

3. Enter the values shown on the following dialog box.

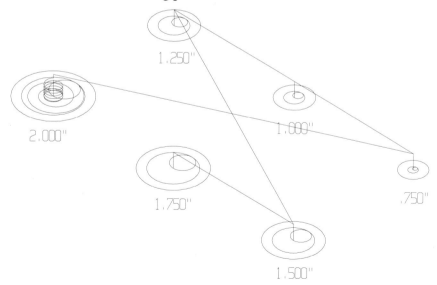

Circle mill roughing

Stepover:	50.0 %	0.25

☑ Helical entry

Minimum radius:	10.0 %	0.05
Maximum radius:	45.0 %	0.225
XY clearance:		0.01
Z clearance:		0.1
Plunge angle:		3.0

☑ Output arc moves

Tolerance: 0.001

If helix fails

○ Plunge   ⦿ Skip

OK   Cancel   Help

4. Choose **OK** twice.

5. Select both operations and regenerate the toolpaths. The toolpath is shown in the following picture:

Exercise 3 – Creating a Thread Mill Toolpath

When creating a thread mill toolpath, you need to define a tool and specify the number of active teeth, speed and feed rates. The resulting toolpath looks like the following picture.

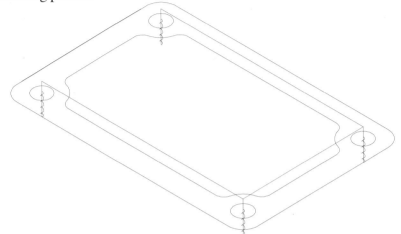

In this exercise you will:

- **Use Toolpaths, Next Menu, Circ tlpths, Thread mill**
- **Define a new tool**

▶ *Open the file and create the toolpath*

1. Open **threadmill.mc8**.

2. Choose
   - **MAIN MENU**
   - **Toolpaths**
   - **Next menu**
   - **Circ tlpths**
   - **Thread mill**

3. Save the NCI file as **threadmill.nci**.

4. Select each of the four circles and choose
   - **Done**
   - **Done**

5. Right-click in the tool display area and select **Create new tool**.

6. Select the **Tool Type** tab, and select the **Bore Bar**.

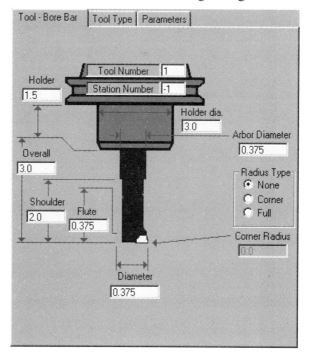

7. Enter the values shown on the following dialog box.

8. Choose **OK** and enter the values shown on the following dialog box.

Tip: Enter the Feed rate, Plunge rate, Retract rate and Spindle speed for the 3/8-inch boring bar tool.

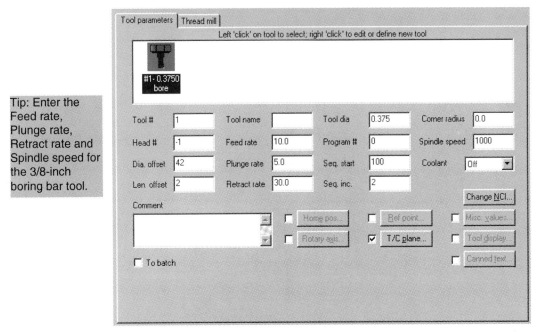

9. Select the **Thread mill** tab.

10. Enter the values shown on the following dialog box.

Tool parameters	Thread mill

Number of active teeth   `1`

Tip: Set the number of active teeth to match the tool.

Clearance plane   `0.25`

Feed plane   `0.1`

Top of thread   `0.0`

Thread depth   `-0.5`

The thread depth determines the number of threads.

○ Absolute   ● Incremental

Thread pitch   `0.05`

Thread start angle   `0.0`

Allowance (overcut)   `0.0`

Compensation in control   `Off ▼`

Entry / exit arc clearance   `0.1`

Entry / exit line length   `0.0`

☑ Helical entry/exit at top of thread
☑ Helical entry/exit at bottom of thread
☐ Linearize helixes

Tolerance   `0.001`

● ID thread
○ OD thread
Major thread diameter   `1.0`

● Right-hand thread
○ Left-hand thread

Machining direction
● Top to bottom
○ Bottom to top
Conventional milling

[OK]   [Cancel]   [Help]

11. Choose **OK**. Mastercam generates the toolpath.

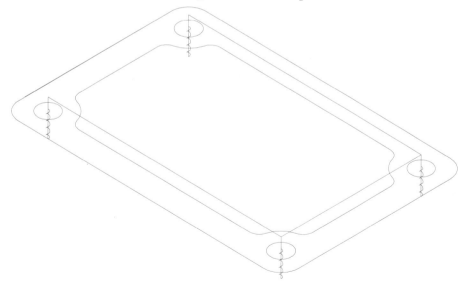

Exercise 4 – Creating a Automatic Drill Toolpath

An automatic drill toolpath automatically selects a tool and other settings and saves time when you create the same toolpath repeatedly for different parts. It is also useful for a part with variously sized drill holes, which this exercise demonstrates.

The final toolpath should look like the following picture:

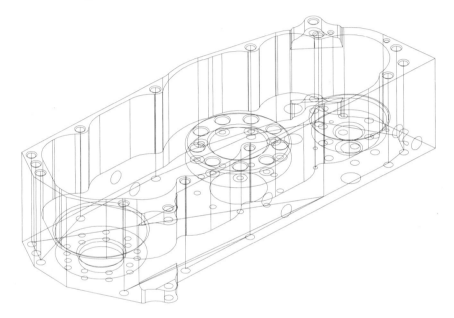

In this exercise, you will:

♦ **Use Toolpaths, Next Menu, Circ tlpths, Auto drill**

♦ **Use pre-drilling**

▶ *Select the arcs for drilling*

1. Open **autodrill.mc8**.

2. Choose

   ♦ **MAIN MENU**

   ♦ **Toolpaths**

   ♦ **Next menu**

   ♦ **Circ tlpths**

   ♦ **Auto drill**

3. Save the NCI file as **autodrill.nci**.

4. *Add arc points.* Choose **Mask on arc**.

5. Select the red arc at position 1 as shown.

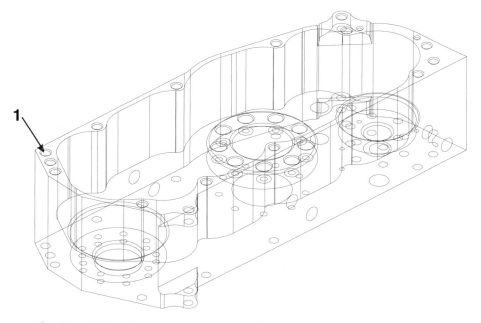

6. Press [Enter] to accept the arc radius matching tolerance.

7. Choose
   ◆ **All**
   ◆ **Arcs**
   ◆ **Done**
   ◆ **Done**

Notice that you do not need to select a tool. The system chooses a tool for each arc, based on the points selected.

▶ *Generate the toolpath*

1. Enter the values shown on the following dialog box.

2. Select the **Depths, Group, and Library** tab.

3. Enter the values shown on the following dialog box.

Tip: For a toolpath with arcs in different views, you can sort operations by view. The sort order appears in the Operations Manager.

4. Select the **Custom Drill Parameters** tab.

5. Enter the values shown on the following dialog box.

6. Select the **Pre-drilling** tab.

7. Enter the values shown on the following dialog box.

8. Choose **OK**. Mastercam generates the toolpath.

Note: Click Yes when asked to accept different tool sizes. To suppress these prompts in the future, you can select "Suppress 'Accept closest matching tool prompts'" on the Tool Parameters tab, as shown in the dialog box in Step 1.

9. Open the Operations Manager and view the operations, which should look like the following picture.

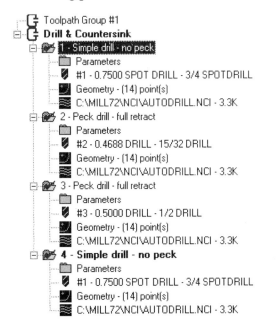

Note: Once operations are generated, you make any modifications by selecting an operation. You do not re-open the Automatic Arc Drilling dialog.

Mastercam generates the following toolpath shown from isometric and top views.

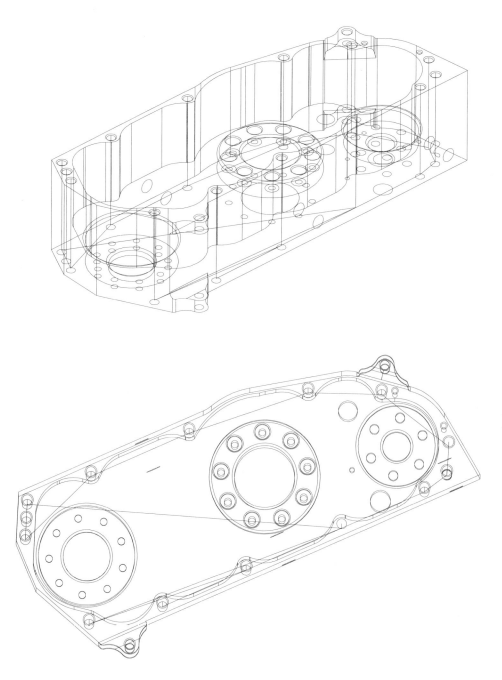

11 *Creating and Machining Surfaces*

This chapter focuses on how to create ruled, loft, and coons surfaces and gives some information about what types of surfaces to create for different wireframe geometry. It introduces surface fillets and demonstrates how setting the surface normals is important to this task. It also shows you some surface toolpaths, including rough parallel, finish parallel, finish leftover, and finish pencil.

Exercise 1 – Creating Surfaces

The following pictures show the wireframe geometry and a shaded image of the completed surfaces used in Exercise 1.

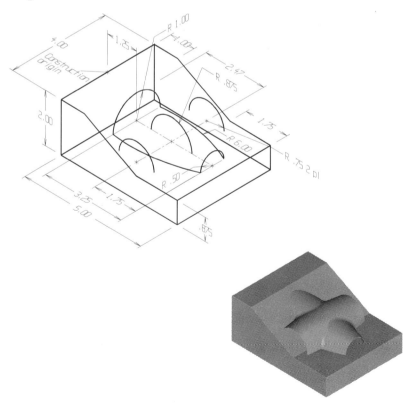

In this exercise, you will:

- **Use the Level Manager**
- **Create a ruled surface**
- **Create a loft surface**
- **Create a coons surface**
- **Create surface fillets**

▶ *Set the level and color for construction*

1. Open **surfaces.mc8**.

2. Choose the **Color** button on the Secondary Menu and set the color to **green (10)**.

3. Choose the **Level** button on the Secondary Menu and set the main level to level **3**, as shown on the right.

Note: All of the wireframe geometry is on level 2 in red.

▶ *Create three ruled surfaces*

1. Choose
- **MAIN MENU**
- **Create**
- **Surface**
- **Ruled**
- **Single**

2. Select the lines at position 1
   and position 2.

Tip: If you used the Chain option
instead of Single, only one ruled
surface with rounded corners would
be created. This would not follow the
shape of the part.

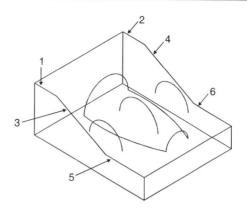

3. Choose
   ◆ **Done**
   ◆ **Do it**

4. Repeat steps 2 and 3 for positions 3 and 4. (Before selecting the lines, choose **Single** to make sure you are using Single chaining.) Then repeat for positions 5 and 6. This creates a total of three ruled surfaces.

5. Choose **BACKUP**.

▶ *Create the loft surface*

1. Choose **Loft**.

2. Select the arcs at positions 1,
   2, and 3 in that order.

Tip: A ruled surface would not work for
this geometry because it would create
sharp corners in the middle of the
surface. A coons surface would not
work because the sections are not
connected.

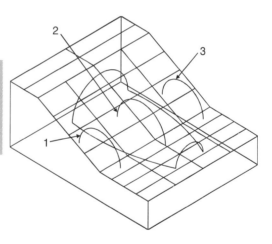

3. Choose
   ◆ **Done**
   ◆ **Do it**

4. Choose **BACKUP**.

▶ *Create the coons surface*

1. Choose **Coons**.

2. When the message shown on the right displays, choose **Yes**.

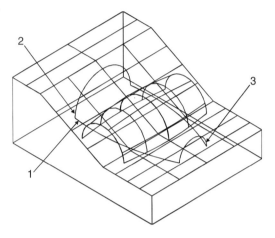

3. *Select Curves which intersect at the upper-left corner.* Select at positions 1 and 2.

4. *Select End of One of the Curves at the lower-right corner.* Select at position 3.

5. Choose **Do it.**

6. Choose **BACKUP**.

7. Press [Alt+S] to see a shaded view of the surfaces. The surfaces should look like the following picture:

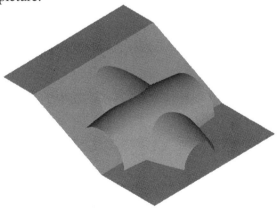

Note: Shading the surfaces makes selection easier when creating surface fillets.

Create surface fillets on the loft and coons surfaces

1. Choose
   - **Fillet**
   - **Surf/surf**

2. *Select first set of surfaces.* Select the loft surface.

3. Choose **Done**.

4. *Select second set of surfaces.* Select the coons surface.

5. Choose **Done**.

6. *Enter the radius.* **.25**

7. Choose **Do it**. The part should look like the following picture.

Note: If the surface fillet is not created, one of the surface normals is probably pointing in the wrong direction.

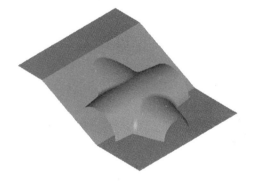

▶ Create surface fillets on two of the ruled surfaces

1. Choose **Surfaces.**

2. *Select first set of surfaces.* Select the top ruled surface.

3. Choose **Done**.

4. *Select second set of surfaces.* Select the next ruled surface.

5. Choose **Done**.

6. *Enter the radius.* **.25**

7. Set the **Trim** option to **Y**.

8. Choose
   - ◆ **Check norms**
   - ◆ **Cycle**
   - ◆ **Flip**
   - ◆ **OK**
   - ◆ **Flip**
   - ◆ **OK**
   - ◆ **Do it**

9. Save the file as **surfaces1.mc8**.

The part should look like the following picture.

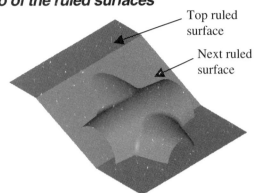

Top ruled surface

Next ruled surface

Tip: The surface normals must point towards the center of the fillet for Mastercam to create the fillet. The arrows for the normals should match the picture below.

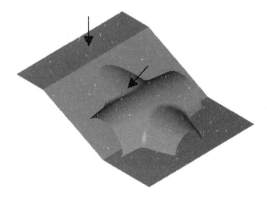

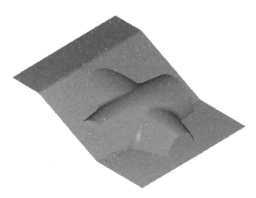

Note: The next procedure is optional - capping the surfaces only improves the aesthetics of the part and does not change the toolpath.

▶ *Cap the ends of the surfaces*

1. Choose
   - ◆ **MAIN MENU**
   - ◆ **Create**
   - ◆ **Surface**
   - ◆ **Trim/extend**
   - ◆ **Flat bndy**
   - ◆ **Manual**

2. Select the coons surface.

3. Drag the arrow cursor to the edge of the surface and click once.

4. Choose
   - ◆ **End here**
   - ◆ **Do it**

5. When the message shown on the right displays, choose **Yes**.

Warning --

? Boundary Curve or Chain is not closed. Want to Automatically Close it?

[Yes]   [No]

6. Choose **Manual**, and repeat steps 2 through 5 for the two ends of the loft surface. The part should look like the following picture.

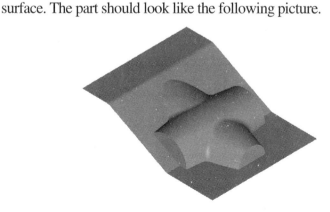

Exercise 2 – Creating a Rough Parallel Toolpath

The rough parallel toolpath removes the bulk of the material quickly. Using a flat endmill instead of a ball endmill also speeds up the material removal. This cutting method does not work well on parts with multiple bosses because the toolpath involves too much plunging. Parallel roughing is the most efficient roughing toolpath for this particular part. The completed toolpath should look like the following picture:

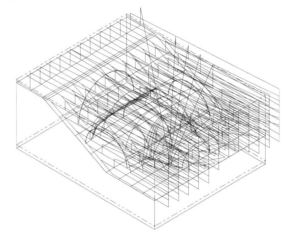

Note: The surfaces do not have to be trimmed in order to be machined. Mastercam automatically cuts only the highest surfaces.

This exercise shows you how to:
- ◆ **Create a rough parallel toolpath**
- ◆ **Use Direction**
- ◆ **Use Cut depths**

▶ *Define the stock boundaries*

1. Open **surfaces1.mc8**.

2. Press [Alt+S] to turn off the shading on the part.

3. Choose
- ◆ **MAIN MENU**
- ◆ **Toolpaths**
- ◆ **Job Setup**

4. Choose the **Select corners** button.

5. Select the geometry at position 1 and position 2.

> Tip: Setting the stock limits is not necessary, but allows for more accurate toolpath verification.

6. Select the **Display stock** check box.

7. Under **Stock Origin**, enter a **Z** value of **0.1**.

8. Choose **OK**.

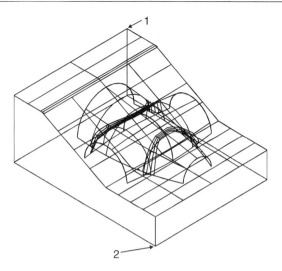

▶ *Select the surfaces for the toolpath and select the tool*

1. Choose
   - ◆ **Surface**
   - ◆ **Rough**
   - ◆ **Parallel**
   - ◆ **Boss**

2. Save the NCI file as **surfaces1.nci**.

3. Choose
   - ◆ **All**
   - ◆ **Surfaces**
   - ◆ **Done**

4. Right-click in the tool display area and select the ½" flat endmill.

▶ *Enter the surface parameters*

1. Select the **Surface parameters** tab.

2. Enter the values as shown on the following dialog box.

3. Choose the **Direction** button.

4. Enter the values shown on the following dialog box.

Tip: Setting a plunge length in the Direction dialog box allows the tool to plunge off the part.

5. Choose **OK**.

► *Enter the rough parallel parameters*

1. Select the **Rough parallel parameters** tab.

2. Enter the values shown on the following dialog box.

Note: Selecting only the Allow positive Z motion along surface option limits the tool motion and prevents the tool from plunging into the material.

3. Choose the **Cut depths** button.

4. Enter the values shown on the following dialog box.

Tip: The adjustment to top cut option sets how far below the top of the surface the first cut lies. The adjustment to other cuts option sets how far above the bottom the last cut lies.

5. Choose **OK** twice.

▶ *Select the tool center boundary and the starting point*

1. *Add Chain: 1.* Choose
   - ◆ **Chain**
   - ◆ **Options**

2. Select the **Plane mask** option and choose **OK**.

3. Select at position 1.

4. Choose **Done**.

5. *Add Chain: 2.* Select at position 2. Mastercam generates the toolpath, which should look like the following wireframe picture. The shaded picture shows what the toolpath looks like after verification.

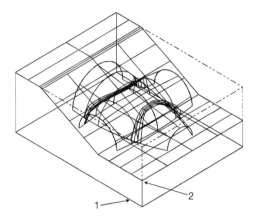

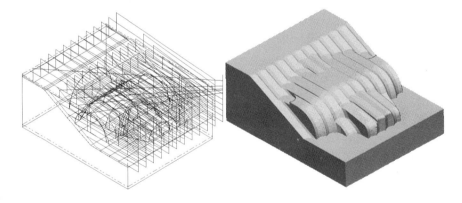

Exercise 3 – Creating a Finish Parallel Toolpath

Using a finish parallel toolpath allows Mastercam to machine over all the surfaces of this part. Parallel finishing is the most efficient choice for this part. The completed toolpath should look like the following picture:

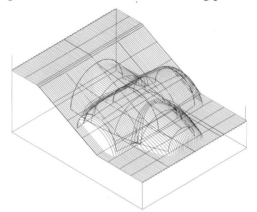

This exercise shows you how to:
- ◆ **Create a finish parallel toolpath**
- ◆ **Use the Filter feature**
- ◆ **Regenerate a surface toolpath**
- ◆ **Use gap settings**

▶ *Select the surfaces for the toolpath and select the tool*

1. Choose
   - ◆ **Finish**
   - ◆ **Parallel**

2. Choose
   - ◆ **All**
   - ◆ **Surfaces**
   - ◆ **Done**

3. Right-click in the tool display area and select the ½" spherical ball endmill.

▶ Enter the surface parameters

1. Select the **Surface parameters** tab.

2. Enter the values as shown on the following dialog box.

3. Choose the **Filter** button.

4. Enter the values shown on the following dialog box.

Tip: The Filter settings eliminate unnecessary lines of NC code from the surface toolpath. Collinear and nearly collinear moves (within a specified tolerance) are removed and arcs are inserted when possible to reduce the toolpath size.

Note: The filter tolerance parameter should be set to a value slightly higher than the original cut tolerance used on the toolpath.

5. Choose **OK**.

► *Enter the finish parallel parameters*

1. Select the **Finish parallel parameters** tab.

2. Enter the values shown on the following dialog box.

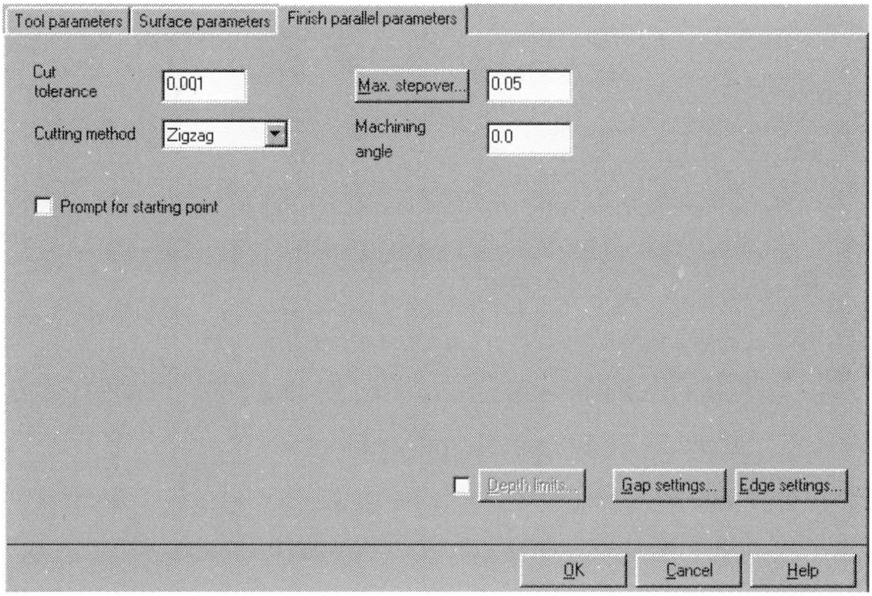

3. Choose **OK**.

4. *Add Chain:1.* Select the same boundary as in Exercise 2.

Note: The plane mask is still active.

5. Choose **Done**. Mastercam generates the toolpath, which should look like the following picture:

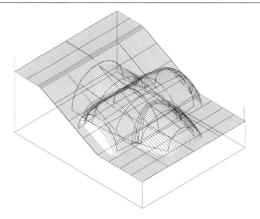

Note: Notice how long this toolpath takes to process. You can reduce the processing time by adjusting the gap settings for the toolpath.

▶ *Change the gap settings*

1. Press [Alt + O] to open the Operations Manager.

2. Select the **Parameters** icon for the Surface Finish Parallel toolpath.

3. Select the **Finish parallel parameters** tab.

4. Choose the **Gap settings** button.

5. Enter the values shown on the following dialog box.

Tip: Setting the gap motion to Smooth creates smooth tool motion between passes. And since the tool motion between passes is on a flat plane, there is no need to check the gap motion for gouges. This setting reduces the time needed to process the toolpath.

Gap settings

Reset

Gap size
- ○ Distance — 0.1
- ⦿ % of stepover — 300.0

Motion < Gap size, keep tool down
- Smooth
- ☐ Check gap motion for gouge

Motion > Gap size, retract
- ☑ Check retract motion for gouge

☐ Optimize cut order

☐ Plunge into previously cut area
☐ Follow tool center boundary at gap

Tangential arc radius: 0.0

Tangential arc angle: 0.0

OK   Cancel   Help

6. Choose **OK** twice.

7. Choose **Regen Path**.

Mastercam generates the toolpath, which should look like the following picture. You should notice a reduction in the processing speed and smooth motion between the passes of the toolpath.

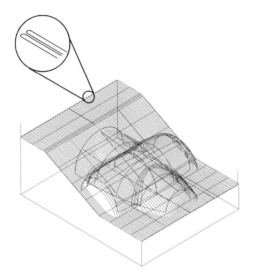

8. Choose **OK** twice.

Exercise 4 – Creating a Finish Leftover Toolpath

The finish leftover toolpath removes material left behind by the larger tool of the finish parallel toolpath. It also adjusts to different Z depths, unlike the Rest Mill option for a surface contour toolpath which can also be used to remove leftover material. The completed toolpath for this exercise should look like the following picture:

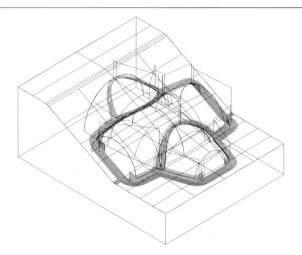

This exercise shows you how to:
- ◆ **Create a finish leftover toolpath**

▶ *Select the surfaces for the toolpath and select the tool*

1. Choose
- ◆ **Surface**
- ◆ **Finish**
- ◆ **Leftover**
- ◆ **All**
- ◆ **Surfaces**
- ◆ **Done**

2. Right-click in the tool display area and select the ¼" spherical ball endmill.

▶ *Enter the surface parameters*

1. Select the **Surface parameters** tab.

2. Enter the values shown on the following dialog box.

▶ *Enter the leftover parameters*

1. Select the **Finish leftover parameters** tab.

2. Enter the values shown on the following dialog box.

3. Choose **OK**. Mastercam generates the toolpath, which should look like the following picture:

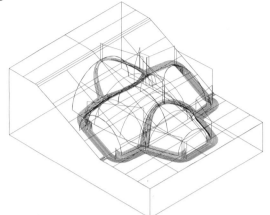

Note: If you receive an error message stating that the toolpath allocation is too low, choose Screen, Configure from the Main Menu and select the Allocations tab. Increase the value for the Toolpath allocation in Kbytes option and choose OK. This increases the amount of RAM designated for toolpath functions.

Exercise 5 – Creating a Finish Pencil Toolpath

On this geometry, the finish pencil toolpath cleans up more of the material by driving the cutter tangent to two surfaces at a time. The completed toolpath for this exercise should look like the following pictures:

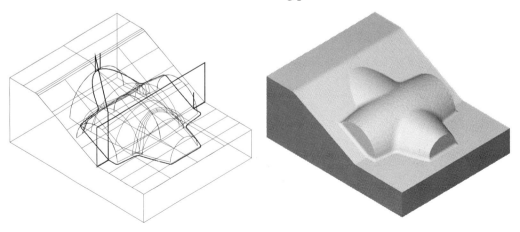

This exercise shows you how to:

- **Create a finish pencil toolpaths**
- **Verify the toolpath**

▶ *Select the surfaces for the toolpath and select the tool*

1. Choose
   - **Finish**
   - **Pencil**

2. Choose
   - **All**
   - **Surfaces**
   - **Done**

3. Right-click in the tool display area and select the 3/16" spherical endmill.

▶ *Enter the surface parameters*

1. Select the **Surface parameters** tab.

2. Enter the values shown on the following dialog box.

| Tool parameters | Surface parameters | Finish pencil parameters |

Clearance... | 2.0 | Tip comp | Tip
○ Absolute ○ Incremental

Retract.. | 0.25 | Stock to leave on drive surfaces | 0.0
○ Absolute ○ Incremental

Feed plane... | 0.5 | ☐ Use check surfaces
○ Absolute ○ Incremental | Stock to leave on check surfaces | 0.0
☑ Rapid retract

Top of stock... | 0.0 | ☐ Prompt for tool center boundary
○ Absolute ○ Incremental

☐ Filter... ☐ Recut... ☐ Direction...

OK | Cancel | Help

▶ *Enter the finish pencil parameters*

1. Select the **Finish pencil parameters** tab.

2. Enter the values shown on the following dialog box.

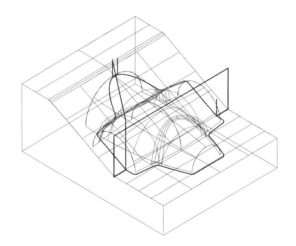

| Tool parameters | Surface parameters | Finish pencil parameters |

Cut tolerance [0.001]

Machining direction
- ◉ Climb
- ○ Conventional

☐ Prompt for starting point

☑ Allow negative Z motion along surface

☑ Allow positive Z motion along surface

☐ Depth limits...   Gap settings...   Edge settings...

OK   Cancel   Help

3. Choose **OK**. Mastercam generates the toolpath, which should look like the following picture:

▶ *Verify all the surface toolpaths*

1. Choose
- ◆ **[ALT + O]**
- ◆ **Select All**
- ◆ **Verify**

2. Choose the **Configuration** button on the Verify toolbar.

3. Enter the values shown on the following dialog box.

Verify configuration: Current MC8		? ✕

Stock

Shape
- ⦿ Box
- ○ Cylinder

Cylinder axis
- ○ X
- ○ Y
- ⦿ Z

Boundaries

	Min point:	Max print:	Margins:
X	0.0	5.0	0.0
Y	-2.0	2.0	0.0
Z	-1.9	0.1	0.0

- Scan NCI file(s)
- Use Job Setup values
- Pick stock corners...

Cylinder diameter: 0.1

- Set colors...
- ☐ Translucent stock

- NCI file
- Current MC8

Tool
- ⦿ Turbo (no tool)
- ○ Wireframe tool
- ○ Solid tool
- ○ Display holder
- ☐ Change tool/color
- ☐ Stop on tool change
- ☐ Stop on gouge

Display control

Moves/step: 10

Moves/refresh: 100000

Speed — Quality

Reset

Miscellaneous
- ☑ Use TrueSolid
- ☐ Cutter compensation in control
- ☐ Display XYZ axes
- ☐ Display coordinates
- ☐ Create log files
- ☐ Compare to STL File

OK   Cancel   Help

4. Choose **OK**.

5. Choose the **Machine** button on the Verify toolbar. Mastercam runs through the toolpaths and displays the verification results, which should look like the following picture:

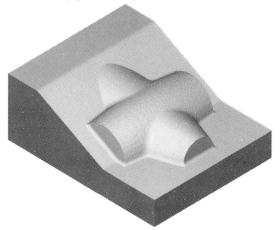

12 *Choosing a Surface Type*

A surface is a 2D or 3D bounded shape that has no thickness. This chapter explains the types of surfaces you can create with Mastercam and shows examples of each type.

Draft

The Draft surface function creates a surface that has angled, or tapered walls defined by a given length and angle. The following picture shows the draft surface that is created from a single chain of curves. You can create this surface type by choosing Create, Surface, Draft from the Main Menu.

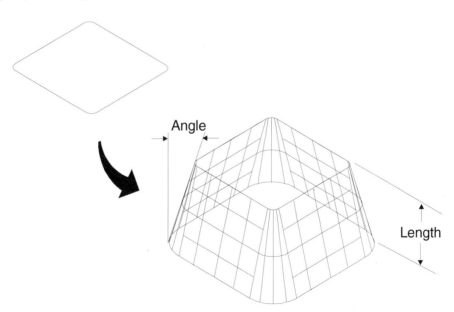

You can also use the Draft surface function to create a chain of curves that contains a single entity.

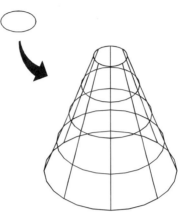

Ruled

The Ruled surface function creates a surface by transitioning between two or more chains of curves in the order that you select them and by using linear blending between each section of the surface. It is important to select each chain of curves at the same relative position to each other. The following picture shows the surface created when you select at positions 1, 2, and 3. You can create this surface type by choosing Create, Surface, Ruled from the Main Menu.

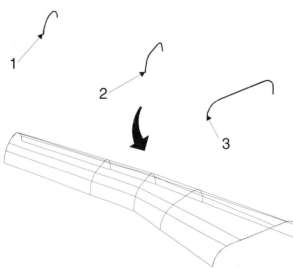

The following picture shows the ruled surface that is created when you select at positions 1 and 2.

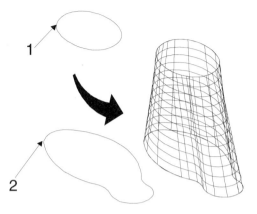

Loft

The Loft surface function creates a surface by transitioning between two or more chains of curves in the order that you select them and calculating a smooth blend by considering all the section chains at once. It is important to select each chain of curves at the same relative position to each other. The following picture shows the surface that is created when you select at positions 1, 2, and 3. Notice the difference between the Loft surface and the Ruled surface on the previous page using the same wireframe geometry. You can create this surface type by choosing Create, Surface, Loft from the Main Menu.

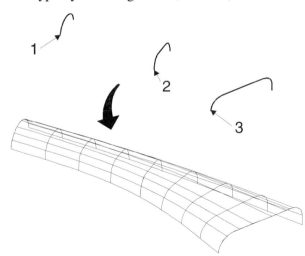

The loft surface shown in the following picture uses 40 cross-sections.

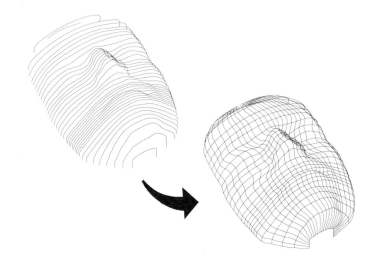

Revolved

The Revolved surface function creates a circular surface by driving the shape of a selected chain of curves about an axis using given start and end angles. Use Revolved when a cross-section and an axis can describe a surface, as shown in the following example. You can create this surface type by choosing Create, Surface, Revolve from the Main Menu.

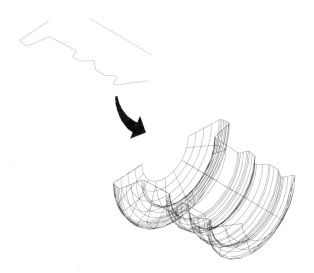

The coffee cup shown in the following picture is another example of a revolved surface.

Note: The handle of the coffee cup is created separately using a different surface function. It is not part of the revolved surface.

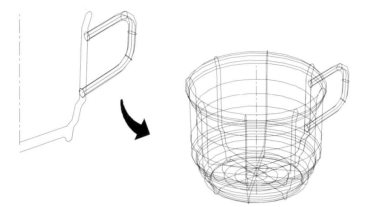

Swept

The Swept surface function creates many different surface configurations depending on the curves that you select. The system sweeps chains of curves called "across contours" over other chains of curves called "along contours." You can select any number of across curves if you are using one along curve. This surface type is shown in the following three pictures. You can create this surface type by choosing Create, Surface, Sweep from the Main Menu.

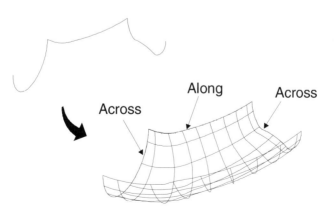

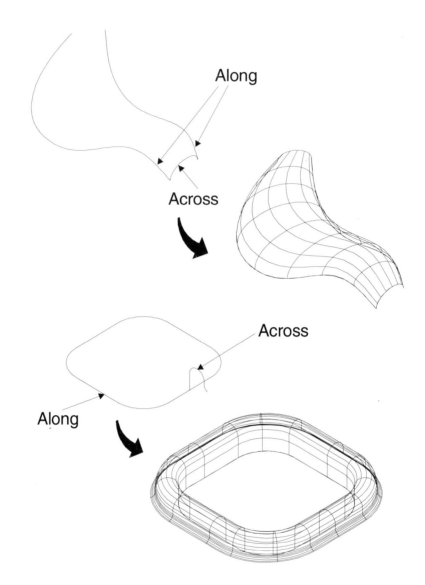

Coons

The Coons surface function creates a surface from a grid of curves. You can create this surface type by choosing Create, Surface, Coons from the Main Menu.

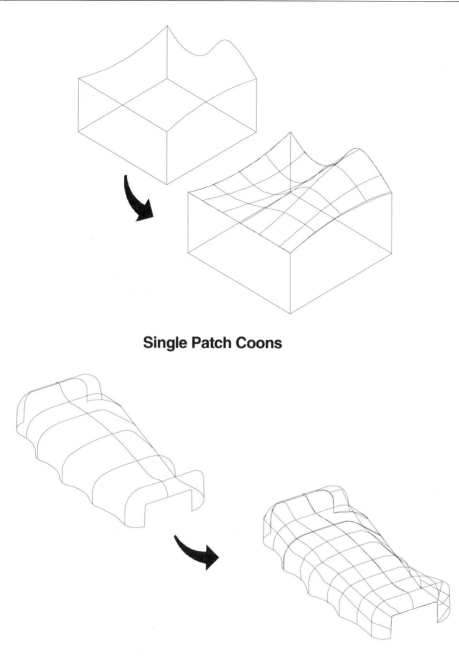

Single Patch Coons

Multiple Patch Coons

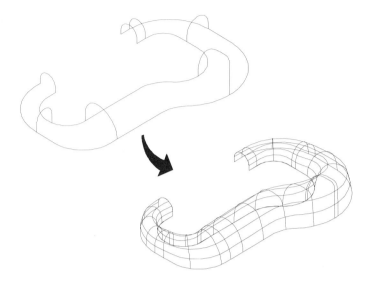

Multiple Patch Coons

Fillet

The Fillet surface function creates a fillet surface, which is mathematically equivalent to a series of arcs and is tangent to one or two surfaces based on the construction method you choose. Fillet surfaces can be created between a plane and a surface, between a curve and a surface, or between two surfaces. You can create this surface type by choosing Create, Surface, Fillet from the Main Menu. The following picture shows a surface to surface fillet example.

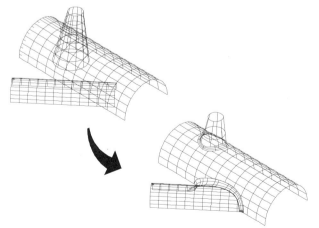

Trim, To surfaces

The Trim, To surfaces surface function trims surfaces to each other. You can create this surface type by choosing Create, Surface, Trim/extend, To surfaces from the Main Menu.

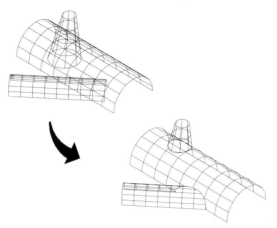

Trim, Flat boundary

The Trim, Flat boundary surface function creates a flat, trimmed surface from one or more planar sets of curves. You can use this surface function to cap the ends of existing surfaces if the wireframe geometry that defines the surface edge exists. You can create this surface type by choosing Create, Surface, Trim/extend, Flat bndy from the Main Menu.

Note: You can select open or closed chains of curves for this surface function. If you select open chains of curves, the system prompts you to close them.

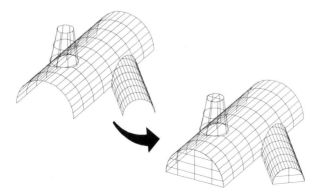

Offset

The Offset surface function creates a surface in which the offset surface is a fixed distance from an existing surface. You can create this surface type by choosing Create, Surface, Offset from the Main Menu.

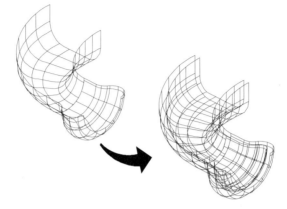

2 Surface Blend

The 2 Surface Blend surface function creates a blended surface between two existing surfaces. This surface type is shown in the following example. You can create this surface type by choosing Create, Surface, Next menu, 2 surf blnd from the Main Menu.

Note: The blend direction and position you set for each selected surface affects the resulting surface.

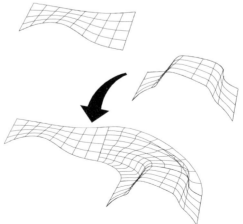

3 Surface Blend

The 3 Surface Blend surface function creates a blended surface between three existing surfaces. You can create this surface type by choosing Create, Surface, Next menu, 3 surf blnd from the Main Menu.

Note: The blend direction and position you set for each selected surface affects the resulting surface.

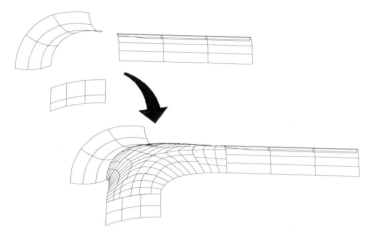

Fillet Blend

The Fillet Blend surface function blends three intersecting fillet surfaces to create one or more blend surfaces. You can create this surface type by choosing Create, Surface, Next menu, Fillet blnd from the Main Menu.

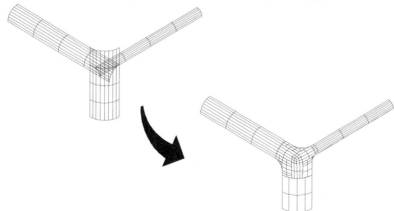

13 *Surface Roughing*

This chapter focuses on some of the roughing toolpaths you can use in surface machining. Roughing toolpaths use large tools to remove the bulk of the material quickly from the part. The rough pocket, rough plunge, rest mill, and high-speed rough pocket toolpaths are shown in this chapter. The rough parallel toolpath is discussed in Chapter 11.

Note: Rough flowline, contour, and radial toolpaths are the same as finish flowline, contour, and radial toolpaths except that roughing allows multiple Z cuts. Finish flowline, contour, and radial toolpaths are covered in Chapter 14.

Exercise 1 – Creating a Rough Pocket Toolpath

Rough pocket toolpaths remove a lot of stock quickly and prepare the part for the finish toolpath. Another benefit of using a rough pocket toolpath on this part is that you can start the toolpath at a point off the part and prevent the tool from plunging into the material. A rough pocket toolpath also creates a series of planar cuts, which is the preferred cutting method for most roughing tools. The geometry for this exercise and the rough pocket toolpath is shown in the following pictures.

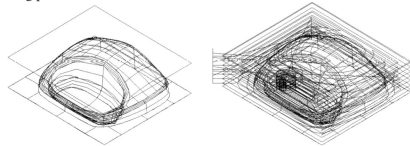

In this exercise, you will:

◆ **Use a Rough Pocket toolpath**
◆ **Use absolute cut depths**
◆ **Use a Constant Overlap Spiral toolpath**

▶ *Select the surfaces for the toolpath and select the tool*

1. Open **roughpocket.mc8.**

2. Choose
   - ◆ **MAIN MENU**
   - ◆ **Toolpaths**
   - ◆ **Surface**
   - ◆ **Rough**
   - ◆ **Pocket**

3. Save the NCI file as **roughpocket.nci.**

4. Choose
   - ◆ **All**
   - ◆ **Surfaces**
   - ◆ **Done**

5. Right-click in the tool display area and select the 3/8" flat endmill.

▶ *Enter the surface parameters*

1. Select the **Surface parameters** tab.

2. Enter the values shown on the following dialog box.

▶ *Enter the pocketing parameters*

1. Select the **Rough pocket parameters** tab.

2. Enter the values shown on the following dialog box.

3. Choose the **Cut depths** button.

4. Enter the values shown on the following dialog box.

Tip: Using absolute cut depths ensures that the toolpath machines between the minimum and maximum depths, although the typical setting is incremental.

5. Choose **OK**.

6. Choose the **Entry - helix** button.

7. Enter the values shown on the following dialog box.

```
Helix/Ramp Parameters                                          ? X

  Helix | Ramp |

    Minimum radius:    26.66667  %  0.1        ┌─Direction──────────────────┐
                                               │   ⦿ CW          ○ CCW      │
    Maximum radius:    266.66667 %  1.0        └────────────────────────────┘

    Z clearance:                    0.2        ┌────────────────────────────┐
                                               │ ☐ Follow boundary          │
    XY clearance:                   0.1        │ ☑ On failure only          │
                                               │   if length exceeds    0.0 │
    Plunge angle:                   3.0        └────────────────────────────┘
                                               ┌─If all entry attempts fail─┐
    ☐ Output arc moves                         │  ⦿ Plunge       ○ Skip     │
                                               │  ☐ Save skipped boundary   │
    Tolerance:                      0.002      └────────────────────────────┘
                                               ┌─Helix feed rate────────────┐
    ☐ Center on entry point                    │  ⦿ Plunge rate  ○ Feed rate│
                                               └────────────────────────────┘

                                         OK         Cancel        Help
```

8. Choose **OK** twice.

9. *Chain outside boundary #1.*
   Select at position 1.

10. Choose **Done**.

Note: For areas that the toolpath cannot use an entry point outside the tool center boundary, it uses a helical entry instead.

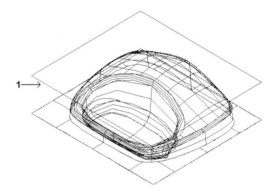

Mastercam completes the toolpath, which should look like the following picture.

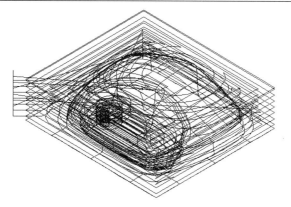

Exercise 2 – Creating a Rough Plunge Toolpath

Rough plunge toolpaths rough a part quickly using a drilling-type motion. Shops that use these toolpaths often invest in special end cutting tools that have a flat bottom to remove stock quickly but can move coolant through the center of the tool to remove chips. Plunge roughing is an appropriate toolpath for deep cavities. The geometry and the roughing toolpath for this exercise are shown in the following pictures.

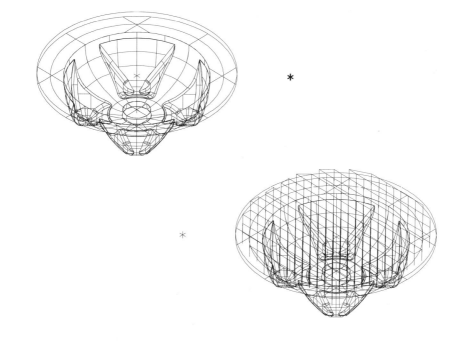

In this exercise, you will:

- ◆ **Use a Rough Plunge toolpath**
- ◆ **Use Cut depths**
- ◆ **Use cylindrical stock in verification**

▶ *Select the surfaces for the toolpath and select the tool*

1. Open **roughplunge.mc8**.

2. Choose
- ◆ **MAIN MENU**
- ◆ **Toolpaths**
- ◆ **Surface**
- ◆ **Rough**
- ◆ **Plunge**

3. Save the NCI file as **roughplunge.nci**.

4. Choose
- ◆ **All**
- ◆ **Surfaces**
- ◆ **Unselect**

5. *Select an entity.* Select at position 1.

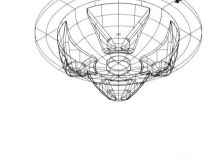

Tip: The selected surface is not machined because a rough plunge toolpath should be used only on areas with a greater Z depth.

6. Press [Esc].

7. Choose **Done**.

8. Right-click in the tool display area and select the 3/8" flat endmill.

▶ *Enter the surface parameters*

1. Select the **Surface parameters** tab.

2. Enter the values shown on the following dialog box.

▶ *Enter the rough plunge parameters*

1. Select the **Rough plunge parameters** tab.

2. Enter the values shown on the following dialog box.

Note: If you set the Maximum stepover parameter too small, the tool moves will overlap and the toolpath includes a lot of air cutting. If you set the stepover too large, the tool deviates from its intended location and not all the material is removed.

3. Choose the **Cut depths** button.

4. Enter the values shown on the following dialog box.

Tip: Setting the cut depths to Absolute and entering values for the minimum and maximum depths that are well below the bottom of the part ensures that the tool goes straight to the bottom of the part and does not use a pecking motion to remove material.

Cut Depths	? X

○ Absolute ○ Incremental

Absolute depths
Minimum depth: -10.0
Maximum depth: -10.0
Select depths...

Incremental depths
Adjustment to top cut: 0.01
Adjustment to other cuts: 0.01
Critical depths...

Relative to: Tip

OK   Cancel   Help

5. Choose **OK** twice.

6. *Select plunge point at lower left.* Select point 1.

7. *Select plunge point at upper right.* Select point 2.

Tip: Selecting the plunge points creates an invisible grid around the part. The toolpath machines within this grid but only where the grid intersects the surfaces of the part. You could select a point in the middle of the part and a point outside the geometry and Mastercam would only rough the area between those two points.

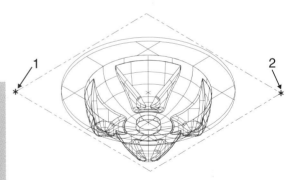

The toolpath should look like the following picture.

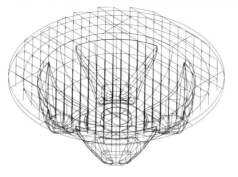

▶ ***Verify the toolpath***

1. Choose [Alt + O] to open the Operations Manager.

2. Choose the **Verify** button.

3. Choose the **Configure** button on the Verify toolbar.

4. Enter the values shown on the following dialog box.

Verify configuration: Current MC8		? ☒

Stock

Shape
- ○ Box
- ⦿ Cylinder

Cylinder axis
- ○ X
- ○ Y
- ⦿ Z

Boundaries

	Min point:	Max point:	Margins:
Scan NCI file(s)			
X	-1.66041	1.64771	0.0
Use Job Setup values			
Y	-1.77756	1.60439	0.0
Pick stock corners...			
Z	-1.12131	0.25	0.0

Cylinder diameter: 4.0

Set colors... ☐ Translucent stock

NCI file
Current MC8

Tool
- ○ Turbo (no tool)
- ⦿ Wireframe tool
- ○ Solid tool
- ○ Display holder
- ☐ Change tool/color
- ☐ Stop on tool change
- ☐ Stop on gouge

Display control

Moves/step: 10
Moves/refresh: 1

Speed ──┼── Quality

Reset

Miscellaneous
- ☐ Use TrueSolid
- ☐ Cutter compensation in control
- ☐ Display XYZ axes
- ☐ Display coordinates
- ☐ Create log files
- ☐ Compare to STL File

OK	Cancel	Help

5. Choose **OK**.

6. Choose the **Machine** button on the Verify toolbar. The verification results should look like the following picture.

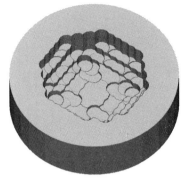

7. Close the Verify toolbar.

8. Choose **OK** to close the Operations Manager.

Exercise 3 – Creating a Rest Mill Toolpath

Rest milling is the only roughing toolpath that cleans up remaining stock with a roughing, planar cut motion. Unlike a finish leftover toolpath that goes directly to the bottom of the remaining stock and risks excessive tool deflection, rest milling identifies the leftover material and effectively removes the stock using multiple Z cuts. The following pictures show the geometry and the rough toolpaths used in this exercise.

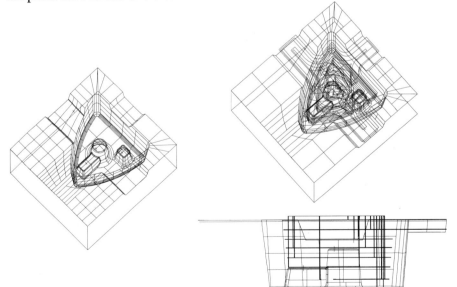

In this exercise, you will:

- ◆ **Use Toolpaths, Surface, Rough, Pocket and Contour**
- ◆ **Use critical depths**

▶ *Select the surfaces for the toolpath and select the tool*

1. Open **restmill.mc8**.

2. Choose

- ◆ **MAIN MENU**
- ◆ **Toolpaths**
- ◆ **Surface**
- ◆ **Rough**
- ◆ **Pocket**

3. Save the NCI file as **restmill.nci**.

4. Choose

- ◆ **All**
- ◆ **Surfaces**
- ◆ **Done**

5. Right-click in the tool display area and select the ¾" flat endmill.

▶ *Enter the surface parameters*

1. Select the **Surface parameters** tab.

2. Enter the values shown on the following dialog box.

▶ Enter the rough pocketing parameters

1. Select the **Rough pocket parameters** tab.

2. Enter the values shown on the following dialog box.

3. Choose the **Entry – helix** button.

4. Enter the values shown on the following dialog box.

5. Choose the **Cut depths** button.

6. Enter the values shown on the following dialog box.

7. Choose the **Critical depths** button.

Tip: Setting critical depths ensures that the toolpath recognizes plateaus in the material. If these plateaus fall between passes, the system inserts an additional pass to clean up the top of the plateau.

8. Select the four points at positions 1 through 4 shown to the right.

9. Press [Esc].

10. Choose **OK** twice.

11. *Chain outside boundary #1.* Choose
    - ◆ **Chain**
    - ◆ **Options**

12. Select the **Plane mask** option and choose **OK**.

13. Select at position 1 as shown to the right.

14. Choose **Done**. Mastercam generates the toolpath.

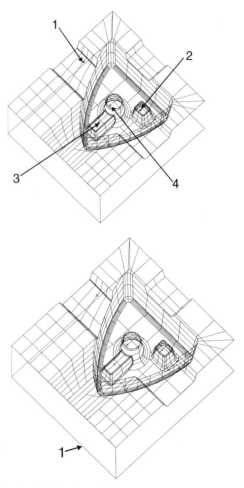

The completed toolpath should look like the following pictures.

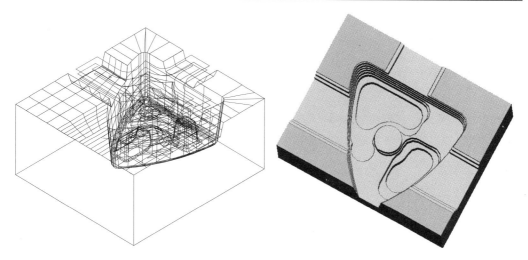

The rough pocket toolpath left areas of material where the ¾" tool could not reach. The rest milling toolpath automatically finds these areas and cleans them out with a smaller tool. Mastercam uses the recut file to establish where the remaining stock lies from the previous rough pocket toolpath.

 Select the surfaces and tool for the rest milling toolpath

1. Choose
   - ◆ **Rough**
   - ◆ **Contour**

2. Choose
   - ◆ **All**
   - ◆ **Surfaces**
   - ◆ **Done**

3. Right-click in the tool display area and select the ¼" flat endmill.

▶ *Enter the surface parameters*

1. Select the **Surface parameters** tab.

2. Enter the values shown on the following dialog box.

▶ *Enter the rough contour parameters*

1. Select the **Rough contour parameters** tab.

2. Enter the values shown on the following dialog box.

3. Choose the **Rest mill** button. The previous operation is selected in the Rest Mill dialog.

4. Enter the values shown on the dialog box at right.

> Tip: The stepover controls the side step distance and the overlap distance determines how far the rest milling toolpath overlaps into the previously cut area.

Rest Mill

Previous operation

Surface Rough Pocket - C:\MILL8\NCI\RESTMILL CR.NCI

Stepover: 0.05

Overlap distance: 0.03

Extension distance: 0.25

OK   Cancel   Help

5. Choose **OK** twice.

6. *Chain outside boundary #1.* Select the same chain as used for the rough pocket toolpath. Mastercam generates the toolpath, which should look like the following pictures.

Note: You could create a new boundary that surrounds just the recut area.

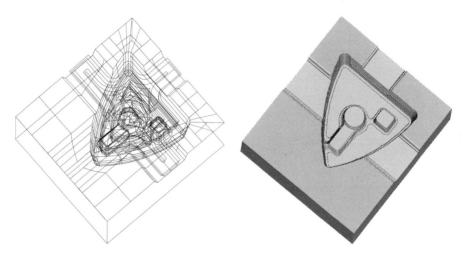

Exercise 4 – High Speed Rough Pocket Toolpath

High speed surface machining is often performed using smooth tool motion, which means that throughout the entire toolpath arcs or small line segments are smoothly connected without sharp corners. It can also include motion that avoids burying the tool in the material. Mastercam includes several options for creating the smoothest possible tool motion between gaps in the toolpath and between depth cuts in the Z axis. You can change the parameters by choosing the High speed button on the Rough contour, Finish contour, or Rough pocket parameters tabs.

The following pictures show the geometry and the rough pocket toolpath used in this exercise.

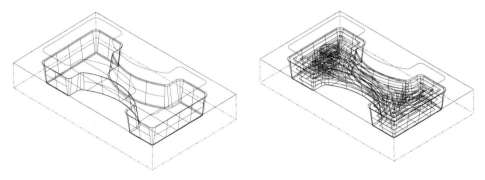

In this exercise, you will:

- ◆ **Use a Rough Pocket toolpath**
- ◆ **Use a High Speed cutting method**

▶ *Select the surfaces for the toolpath and select the tool*

1. Open **highspeed.mc8**.

2. Choose
   - ◆ **MAIN MENU**
   - ◆ **Toolpaths**
   - ◆ **Surface**
   - ◆ **Rough**
   - ◆ **Pocket**

3. Save the NCI file as **highspeed.nci**.

4. Choose
   - ◆ **All**
   - ◆ **Surfaces**
   - ◆ **Done**

5. Right-click in the tool display area and select the ½" flat endmill.

▶ *Enter the surface parameters*

1. Select the **Surface parameters** tab.

2. Enter the values shown on the following dialog box.

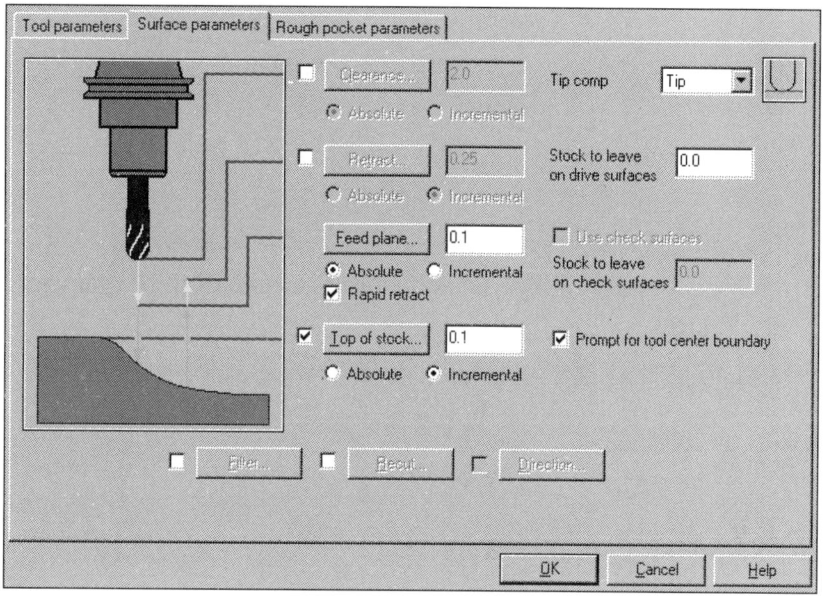

▶ *Enter the rough pocket parameters*

1. Select the **Rough pocket parameters** tab.

2. Enter the values shown on the following dialog box.

3. Choose the **Entry - helix** button. The Helix/Ramp Parameters dialog opens.

4. Enter the values shown on the following dialog box.

5. Choose **OK**.

6. Choose the **Cut depths** button. The Cut Depths dialog box opens.

7. Enter the values shown on the following dialog box and choose **OK**.

8. Choose the **Gap settings** button. The Gap settings dialog box opens.

9. Enter the values shown on the dialog box to the right and choose **OK**.

10. Choose the **Edge settings** button. The Edge settings dialog box opens.

11. Enter the values shown on the dialog box to the right and choose **OK**.

Edge settings	?	X

Reset

Roll tool
- ⦿ Automatically
- ○ Only between surfaces
- ○ Over all surface edges

Sharp corner tolerance
- ○ Distance   0.001
- ⦿ % of cut tolerance   100.0

OK   Cancel   Help

12. Choose **OK** twice.

13. Select the yellow geometry above the pocket as shown at position 1 in the picture to the right.

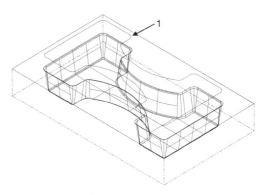

14. Choose **Done**. Mastercam completes the toolpath, which should look like the following picture. The toolpath uses high speed loops and channel cuts to machine the part.

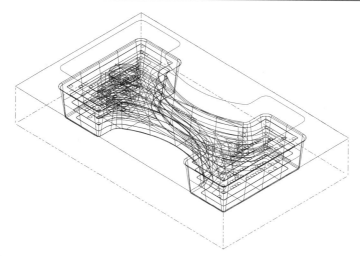

The following picture shows only the first depth cut of the toolpath.

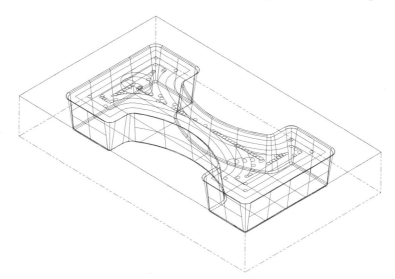

14 *Surface Finishing*

This chapter focuses on some of the finishing toolpaths you can use in surface machining. Finish toolpaths can be used to remove material left behind by previous roughing toolpaths. The finish parallel steep, radial, project, flowline, contour, shallow, and scallop toolpaths are shown in this chapter. The finish parallel, leftover, and pencil toolpaths are discussed in Chapter 11.

Exercise 1 –Using Finish Steep and Shallow

Using finish steep and shallow toolpaths on the part below makes sense because a finish parallel toolpath would miss material in the steep areas of the part and a finish contour toolpath would miss material in the shallow areas of the part (see the pictures below). A finish parallel steep toolpath is usually used after a finish parallel toolpath.

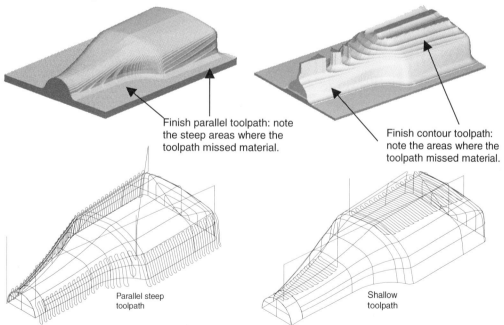

Finish parallel toolpath: note the steep areas where the toolpath missed material.

Finish contour toolpath: note the areas where the toolpath missed material.

Parallel steep toolpath

Shallow toolpath

In this exercise, you will:

- ◆ **Use Toolpaths, Surface, Finish, Parallel steep**
- ◆ **Use Toolpaths, Surface, Finish, Shallow**
- ◆ **Use Gap settings, tangential arcs**

▶ *Select the surfaces for the steep toolpath and select the tool*

1. Open **steepshallow.mc8**.

2. Choose
   - ◆ **MAIN MENU**
   - ◆ **Toolpaths**
   - ◆ **Surface**
   - ◆ **Finish**
   - ◆ **Par. Steep**

3. Save the NCI file as **steepshallow.nci**.

4. Choose
   - ◆ **All**
   - ◆ **Surfaces**
   - ◆ **Done**

5. Right-click in the tool display area and select the ¼" spherical ball endmill.

▶ *Enter the surface parameters*

1. Select the **Surface parameters** tab.

2. Enter the values shown on the following dialog box.

▶ *Enter the finish parallel steep parameters*

1. Select the **Finish parallel steep parameters** tab.

2. Enter the values shown on the following dialog box.

3. Choose the **Gap settings** button.

4. Enter the values shown on the dialog box at right.

> Tip: Tangential arcs are useful in steep and shallow toolpaths where you cut a previously finished surface. They allow the system to blend the entry and exit moves for each cut.

5. Choose **OK** twice.

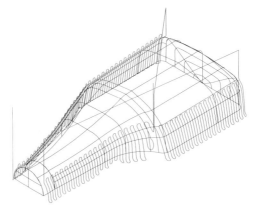

Mastercam generates the steep toolpath on the areas of the part between 50 and 90 degrees. The toolpath should look like the following picture:

▶ *Select the surfaces for the shallow toolpath and select the tool*

1. Choose
   - ◆ **MAIN MENU**
   - ◆ **Toolpaths**
   - ◆ **Surface**
   - ◆ **Finish**

♦ **Shallow**
♦ **All**
♦ **Surfaces**
♦ **Done**

2. Select the same ¼" spherical endmill used for the parallel steep toolpath.

▶ *Enter the surface parameters*

1. Select the **Surface parameters** tab.

2. Enter the values shown on the following dialog box.

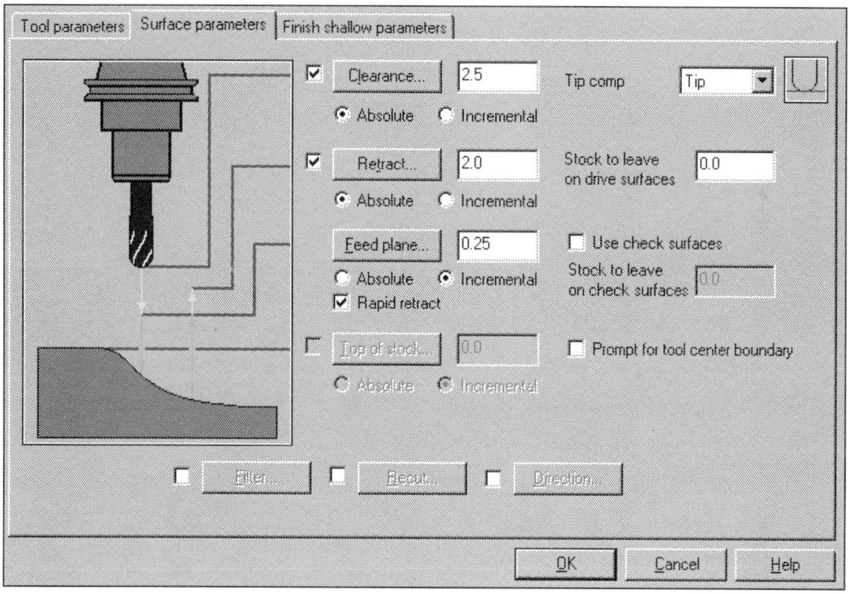

▶ *Enter the finish shallow parameters*

1. Select the **Finish shallow parameters** tab.

2. Enter the values shown on the following dialog box.

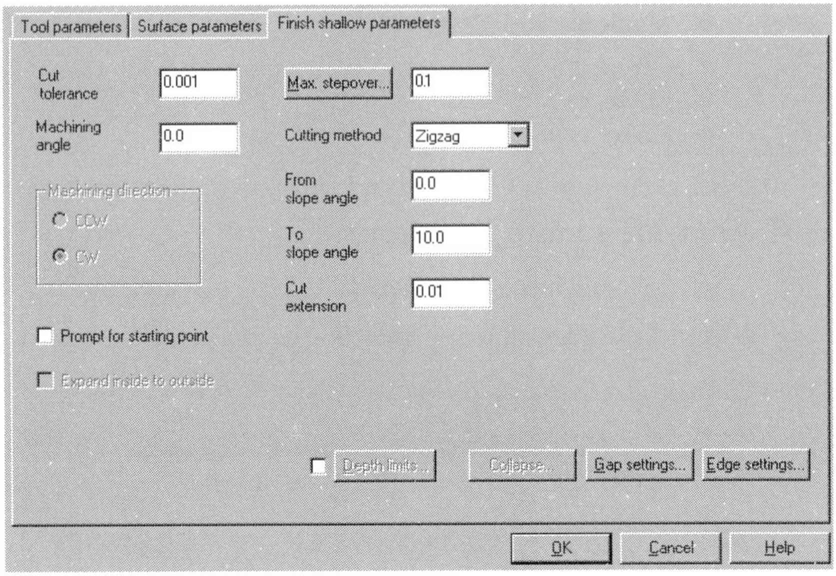

3. Choose the **Gap settings** button.

4. Enter the values shown on the dialog box at right.

5. Choose **OK** twice. Mastercam generates the shallow toolpath on the areas of the part between 0 and 10 degrees. The toolpath should look like the following picture.

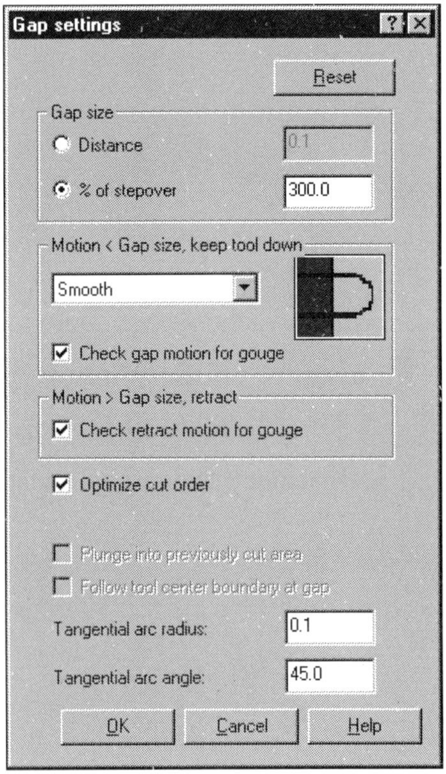

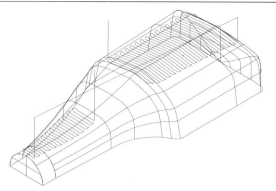

Exercise 2 – Creating a Finish Radial Toolpath

Finish radial toolpaths can sometimes be the most efficient toolpaths for round parts. The geometry and the finish toolpath for this exercise are shown in the following pictures:

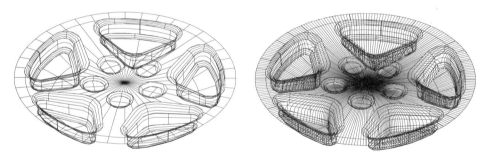

In this exercise, you will:

- ◆ **Use Toolpaths, Surface, Finish, Radial**

▶ *Select the surfaces for the toolpath and select the tool*

1. Open **radial.mc8.**

2. Choose
   - ◆ **MAIN MENU**
   - ◆ **Toolpaths**
   - ◆ **Surface**
   - ◆ **Finish**
   - ◆ **Radial**

3. Save the NCI file as **radial.nci**.

4. Choose

◆ **All**

◆ **Surfaces**

◆ **Done**

5. Right-click in the tool display area and select the ¼" spherical ball endmill.

 Enter the surface parameters

1. Select the **Surface parameters** tab.

2. Enter the values shown on the following dialog box.

| Tool parameters | Surface parameters | Finish radial parameters |

☐ Clearance... 2.5   Tip comp [Tip ▾]

    ◉ Absolute   ○ Incremental

☐ Retract... 2.0   Stock to leave [0.0]
       on drive surfaces

    ○ Absolute   ○ Incremental

Feed plane... [0.25]   ☐ Use check surfaces

○ Absolute   ◉ Incremental   Stock to leave [0.0]
☑ Rapid retract   on check surfaces

☐ Top of stock... 0.0   ☐ Prompt for tool center boundary

    ○ Absolute   ◉ Incremental

☐ Filter...   ☐ Recut...   ☐ Direction...

[OK]   [Cancel]   [Help]

▶ *Enter the finish radial parameters*

1. Select the **Finish radial parameters** tab.

2. Enter the values shown on the following dialog box.

| Tool parameters | Surface parameters | Finish radial parameters |

| Cut tolerance | 0.001 | Max. angle increment | 1.5 | Start offset distance | 0.01 |
| Cutting method | Zigzag ▼ | Start angle | 0.0 | Sweep angle | 360.0 |

Starting point
- ⦿ Start inside
- ○ Start outside

☐ Depth limits   Gap settings...   Edge settings...

OK   Cancel   Help

Note: If this part had a hole in the center, you could use the start offset distance to offset the center of the toolpath from the hole. This would reduce the retract moves in the radial toolpath.

3. Choose **OK**.

4. *Enter an approximate starting point.* Select point 1. Mastercam generates the toolpath, which should look like the following pictures:

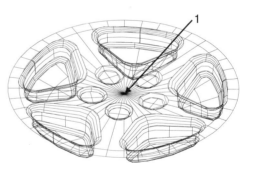

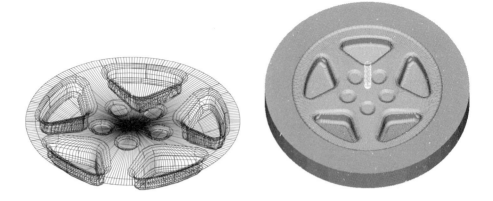

Exercise 3 – Creating a Finish Project Toolpath

Finish project toolpaths project an NCI file or entities onto selected surfaces. This finish toolpath provides free-form motion with the capability to match the cut motion closely to the shape of the part. It also provides the most tool control. Engraving machining often uses project toolpaths. The part and the finish toolpath for this exercise are shown in the following pictures:

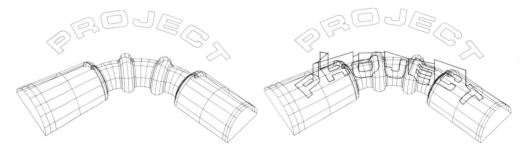

In this exercise, you will:

◆ **Use Toolpaths, Surface, Finish, Project**

▶ *Select the surfaces for the toolpath and select the tool*

1. Open **project.mc8**.

2. Choose

    ◆ **MAIN MENU**

    ◆ **Toolpaths**

    ◆ **Surface**

◆ **Finish**
◆ **Project**

3. Save the NCI file as **project.nci**.

4. Choose
◆ **All**
◆ **Surfaces**
◆ **Done**

5. Right-click in the tool display area and select the 1/32" flat endmill.

▶ *Enter the surface parameters*

1. Select the **Surface parameters** tab.

2. Enter the values shown on the following dialog box.

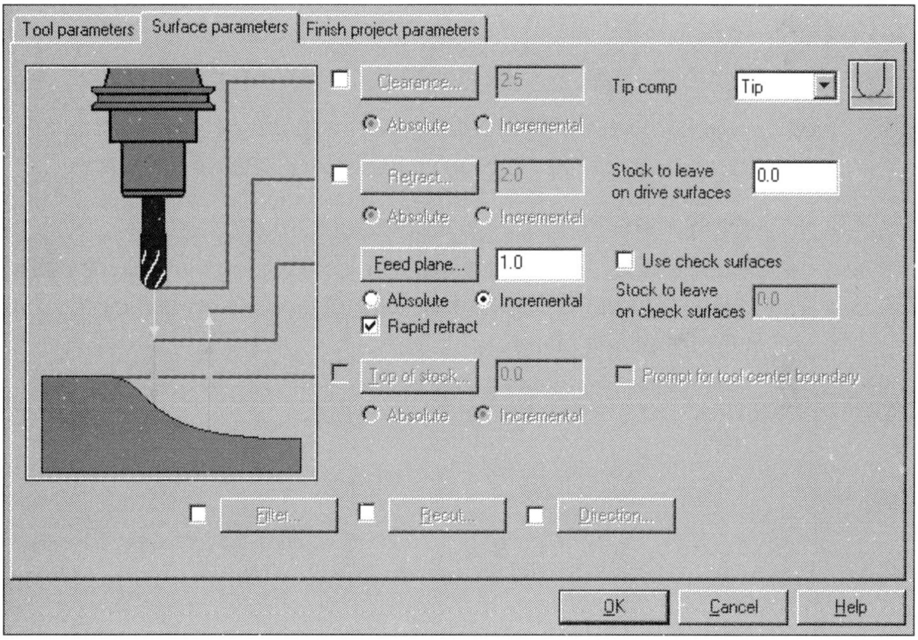

▶ *Enter the finish project parameters*

1. Select the **Finish project parameters** tab.

2. Enter the values shown on the following dialog box.

| Tool parameters | Surface parameters | Finish project parameters |

Cut tolerance: `0.001`

Projection type
- ○ NCI
- ● Curves
- ○ Points

☐ Add depths

Source operation

☐ Depth limits...   Gap settings...   Edge settings...

OK   Cancel   Help

Note: If you had previously created other toolpaths, you could select the toolpaths you wanted to project from the Source operation list area.

3. Choose **OK**.

4. Chain each section of the word "project" beginning with the outside boundary of the "P." Continue selecting the chains in the order displayed in the following picture.

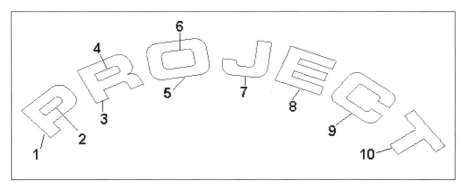

5. Choose **Done**. Mastercam generates the toolpath, which should look like the following picture:

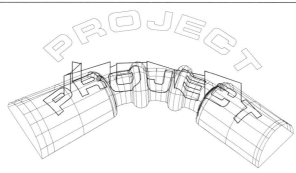

Exercise 4 – Using a Finish Flowline Toolpath

Finish flowline toolpaths follow the shape and direction of the surfaces and create a smooth and flowing toolpath motion. A finish parallel toolpath machines the part at a set angle and does not flow with the surfaces, resulting in a lot of air cutting. The geometry and the finish toolpath for this exercise are shown in the following pictures:

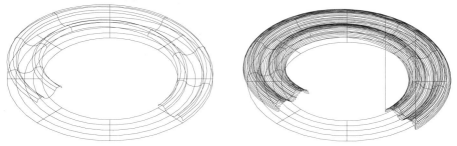

In this exercise, you will:

◆ **Use Toolpaths, Surface, Finish, Flowline**
◆ **Use Flowline menu, cut direction**

▶ *Select the surfaces for the toolpath and select the tool*

1. Open **flowline.mc8**.

2. Choose
   ◆ **MAIN MENU**
   ◆ **Toolpaths**
   ◆ **Surface**
   ◆ **Finish**
   ◆ **Flowline**

3. Save the NCI file as
   flowline.nci.

4. *Select surfaces*. Select the red
   surface at position 1.

5. Choose **Done**. The Flowline
   menu displays.

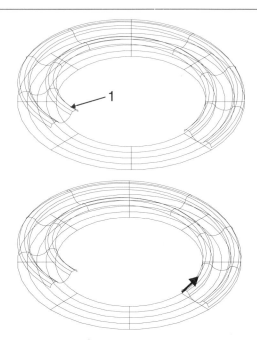

6. Choose **Cut dir**. The arrow
   indicating the cut direction of
   the toolpath should change to
   match the picture shown on
   the right.

7. Choose **Do it**.

8. Right-click in the tool display area and select the 3/16" spherical ball
   endmill.

▶ *Enter the surface parameters*

1. Select the **Surface parameters** tab.

2. Enter the values shown on the following dialog box.

▶ Enter the finish flowline parameters

1. Select the **Finish flowline parameters** tab.

2. Enter the values shown on the following dialog box.

3. Choose **OK**.

Mastercam generates the toolpath, which should look like the following picture:

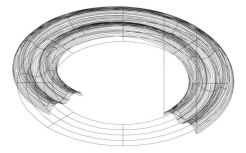

The following picture shows another part where a flowline toolpath is appropriate.

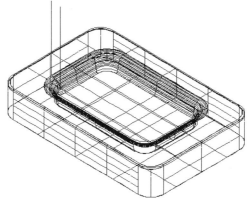

Exercise 5 – Using a Finish Contour Toolpath

Finish contour works well for the following part because the part includes several steep walls. The finish contour toolpath allows the tool to step down gradually in the Z axis instead of stepping over in the X and Y axes. The part and the finish toolpath for this exercise are shown in the following pictures.

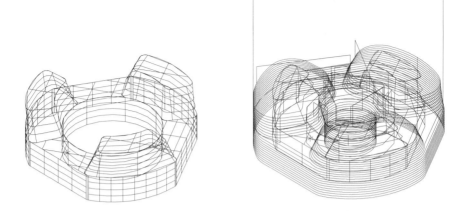

In this exercise, you will:
- ◆ **Use Toolpaths, Surface, Finish, Contour**
- ◆ **Use Critical depths**

▶ *Select the surfaces for the toolpath and select the tool*

1. Open **contour.mc8**.

2. Choose
- ◆ **MAIN MENU**
- ◆ **Toolpaths**
- ◆ **Surface**
- ◆ **Finish**
- ◆ **Contour**

3. Save the NCI file as **contour.nci**.

4. Choose
- ◆ **All**
- ◆ **Surfaces**
- ◆ **Done**

5. Right-click in the tool display area and select the ¾" bull-nose endmill with the 1/8" corner radius.

▶ *Enter the surface parameters*

1. Select the **Surface parameters** tab.

2. Enter the values shown on the following dialog box.

▶ *Enter the contour parameters*

1. Select the **Finish contour parameters** tab.

2. Enter the values shown on the following dialog box.

Note: The ramp length determines the size of the ramp between the constant Z depth cuts. This provides smooth motion between depth cuts, allowing for higher feed rates.

3. Choose the **Cut depths** button.

4. Enter the values shown on the following dialog box.

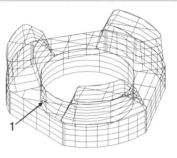

5. Choose the **Critical depths** button.

Tip: Using critical depths ensures that the tool makes a cut at the specified depth.

6. Select the red point at position 1.

7. Press [Esc]. The depth of the point displays in the Critical depths text box, as shown on the following dialog box.

8. Choose **OK**.

9. Choose the **Gap settings** button.

10. Enter the values shown on the dialog box at right.

11. Choose **OK**.

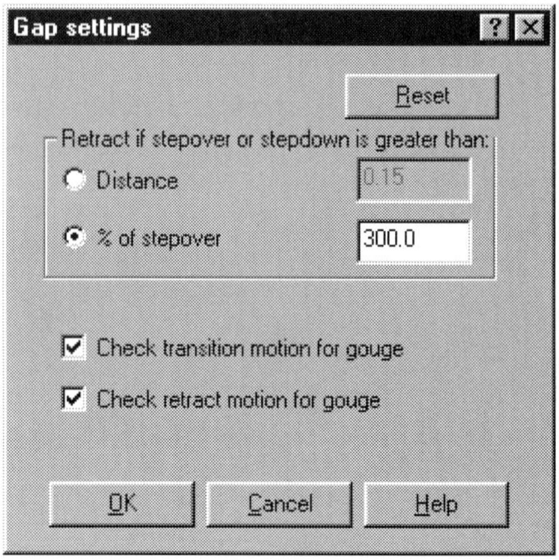

Gap settings

Reset

Retract if stepover or stepdown is greater than:

○ Distance [0.15]

◉ % of stepover [300.0]

☑ Check transition motion for gouge

☑ Check retract motion for gouge

[OK] [Cancel] [Help]

12. Choose the **Edge settings** button.

13. Enter the values shown on the dialog box at right.

Tip: Setting the tool to roll over all surface edges results in better vertical wall recognition. Only the edge of a vertical wall is seen as an edge from the top, so this setting may be necessary in order for the vertical wall to be cut.

Edge settings

Reset

Roll tool
○ Automatically
○ Only between surfaces
◉ Over all surface edges

Sharp corner tolerance
○ Distance [0.001]
◉ % of cut tolerance [100.0]

[OK] [Cancel] [Help]

14. Choose **OK** twice. Mastercam generates the toolpath, which should look like the following pictures. The bottom picture shows the constant Z moves in more detail.

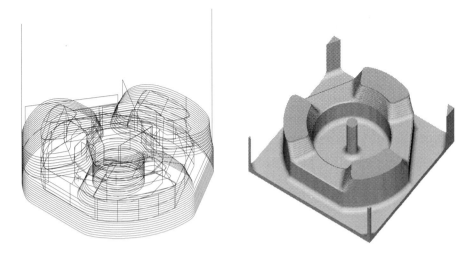

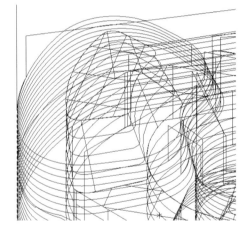

Exercise 6 – Using a Finish Scallop Toolpath

For the part in this exercise, finish scallop creates a consistent scallop height over the whole part regardless of whether the surface becomes steep or shallow. Mastercam creates the consistent scallop height without having to double up on the step size in the steep areas. The part and the finish toolpath for this exercise are shown in the following pictures.

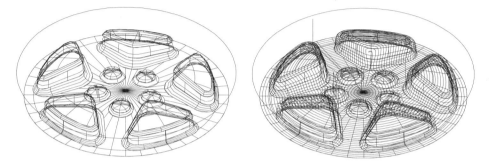

In this exercise, you will:

- ◆ **Use Toolpaths, Surface, Finish, Scallop**
- ◆ **Use Collapse resolution**
- ◆ **Use Gap settings**

▶ *Select the surfaces for the toolpath and select the tool*

1. Open **scallop.mc8**.

2. Choose
   - ◆ **MAIN MENU**
   - ◆ **Toolpaths**
   - ◆ **Surface**
   - ◆ **Finish**
   - ◆ **Scallop**

3. Save the NCI file as **scallop.nci**.

4. Choose
   - ◆ **All**
   - ◆ **Surfaces**
   - ◆ **Done**

5. Right-click in the tool display area and select the ¼" spherical ball endmill.

▶ *Enter the surface parameters*

1. Select the **Surface parameters** tab.

2. Enter the values shown on the following dialog box.

▶ *Enter the finish scallop parameters*

1. Select the **Finish scallop parameters** tab.

2. Enter the values shown on the following dialog box.

3. Choose the **Collapse** button.

4. Enter the values shown on the dialog box at right.

Tip: The collapse resolution defines how smoothly the collapse zones of the 3D collapse toolpath are created. The system uses the stepover percentage to create a "mesh" over the surfaces that determines where the toolpath is placed. A smaller collapse resolution creates a tighter mesh and a more accurate toolpath, but it also takes longer to generate and makes a longer NC program.

5. Choose **OK**.

6. Choose the **Gap settings** button.

7. Enter the values shown on the dialog box at right.

Gap settings

Reset

Gap size
- ○ Distance [0.1]
- ● % of stepover [300.0]

Motion < Gap size, keep tool down
[Smooth ▼]

☐ Check gap motion for gouge

Motion > Gap size, retract
☑ Check retract motion for gouge

☑ Optimize cut order

☐ Plunge into previously cut area
☐ Follow tool center boundary at gap

Tangential arc radius: [0.0]

Tangential arc angle: [0.0]

OK | Cancel | Help

8. Choose **OK** twice. Mastercam generates the toolpath, which should look like the following pictures:

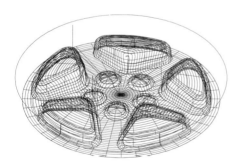

Exercise 7 – Creating a Contour Shallow Toolpath

The contour shallow function gives you more control of the tool motion in shallow areas of a part. You can use this toolpath to reduce or increase the number of cuts in these areas. The cuts added to the shallow area can be partial or complete. A partial cut would cause tool motion to be added in only the shallow areas while a complete cut would cause tool motion to be added in shallow areas and possibly some steeper areas. The part and finished toolpath should look like the following pictures:

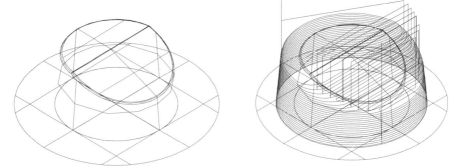

In this exercise, you will:

- **Use Toolpaths, Surface, Finish, Contour**
- **Use the Contour Shallow function**

▶ *Open the file and select surfaces*

1. Open **addcuts.mc8**.

2. Choose
    - **Toolpaths**
    - **Surface**
    - **Finish**
    - **Contour**

3. Save the NCI file as **addcuts.nci**.

4. Choose
    - **All**
    - **Surfaces**
    - **Done**

5. Right-click in the tool display area and select the ¾ " flat endmill.

▶ *Enter the surface parameters*

1. Select the **Surface parameters** tab.

2. Enter the values shown on the following dialog box.

▶ *Enter the finish contour parameters*

1. Select the **Finish contour parameters** tab.

2. Enter the values shown on the following dialog box.

3. Choose the **Shallow** button.

4. Enter the values shown on the following dialog box.

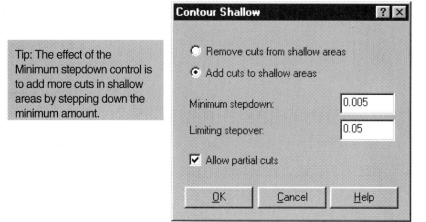

Tip: The effect of the Minimum stepdown control is to add more cuts in shallow areas by stepping down the minimum amount.

5. Click **OK** twice. Mastercam generates the toolpath, which should look like the following picture:

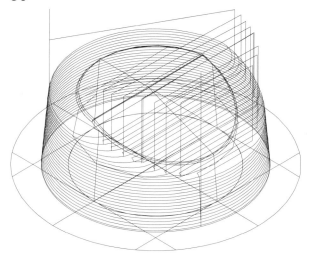

15 *Creating a Multiaxis Toolpath*

A multiaxis toolpath can be a 3-, 4-, or 5-axis toolpath. These toolpaths are used for parts that have surfaces and/or curves. With a 3-axis toolpath, you can machine the part on one side, turn it over, and machine the other side. With a 5-axis toolpath, you can machine the part without having to turn the part over manually. This chapter shows you how to create different types of multiaxis toolpaths for appropriately shaped 3D parts.

Exercise 1 – Creating a Curve 5-Axis Toolpath with 3-axis output

This exercise shows you how to use 3D curves as an option in a 5-axis toolpath. This toolpath is useful for a part with curved surfaces because it allows for precise tool tip control. The part in this example, a blade and root part, has curved surfaces. Unlike the 3-axis contour toolpath, the curve 5-axis toolpath allows for more precise contact between the tool and the surface material.

The geometry and toolpath are shown in the following picture.

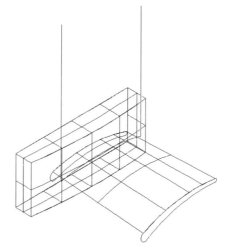

This exercise shows you how to create a multiaxis toolpath. You learn how to:

◆ **Use Toolpaths, Multiaxis, Curve5ax**

▶ *Select the surfaces for the toolpath*

1. Open **curve5.mc8**.

2. Choose
   ◆ **MAIN MENU**
   ◆ **Toolpaths**
   ◆ **Multiaxis**
   ◆ **Curve5ax**

3. Save the NCI file as **curve5.nci**.

4. Enter the values shown on the following dialog box.

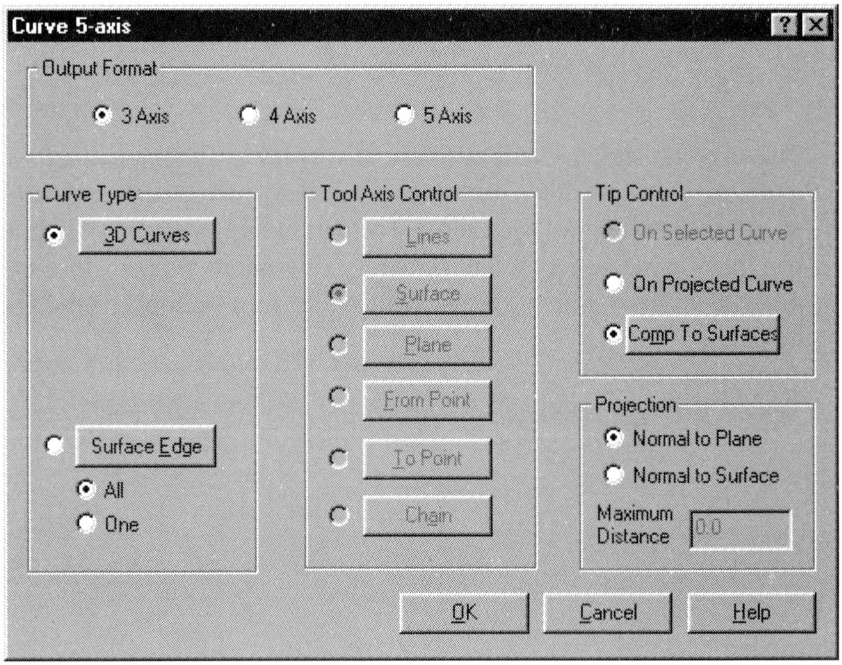

5. Choose the **3D Curves** button. (The dialog box closes temporarily to allow you to select surfaces.)

6. *Select Tool Axis surface(s)*. Select at position 1.

7. Choose
   - ◆ **Done**
   - ◆ **Single**

8. *Chain boundaries*. Select at position 2.

9. Choose **Done**.

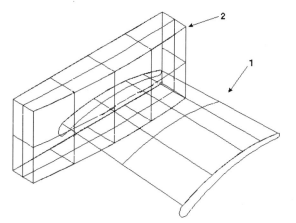

10. The Curve5-axis dialog box reappears. Choose the **Comp to Surfaces** button.

11. *Select Compensation surface(s)*. Select at position 1 (as shown above).

12. Choose **Done**.

13. The Curve5-axis dialog box reappears. Now that all surfaces have been selected, choose **OK**.

▶ Select the tool and enter the multiaxis and curve 5-axis parameters

1. Right-click in the tool display area and select the ½" bull endmill with the .125 corner radius.

2. Select the **Multiaxis parameters** tab.

3. Enter the values shown on the following dialog box.

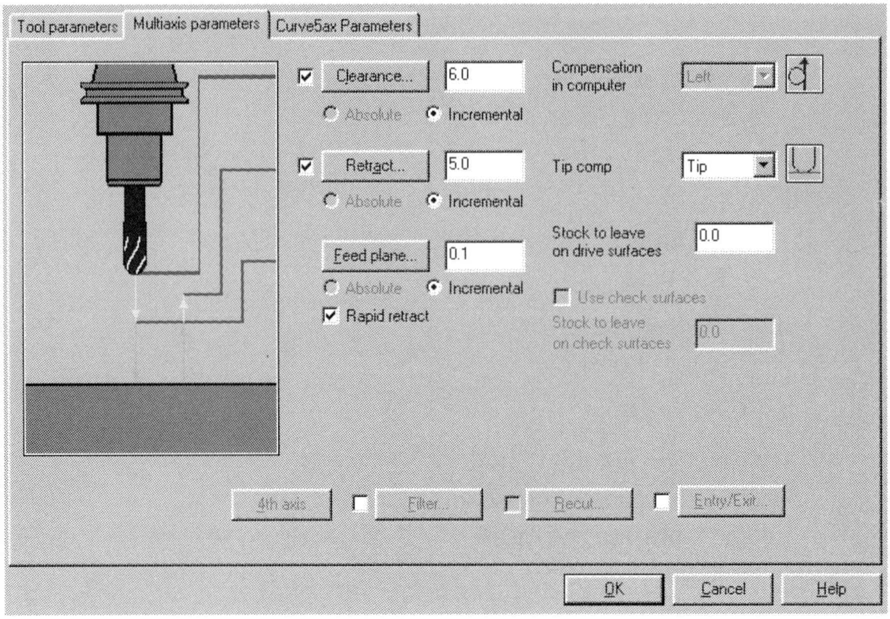

4. Select the **Curve5ax Parameters** tab.

5. Enter the values shown on the following dialog box.

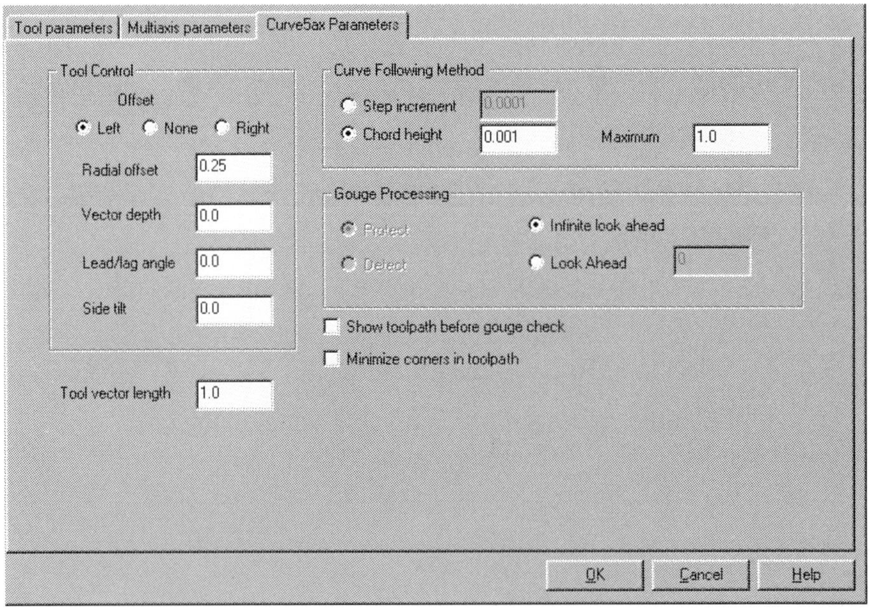

6. Choose **OK**. Mastercam generates the toolpath, which should look like the following picture.

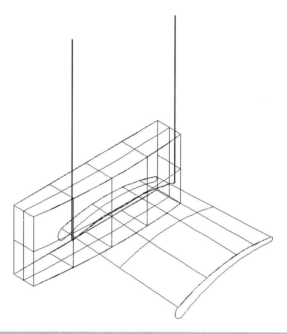

Exercise 2 – Creating a Smooth Entry and Exit

The toolpath for the blade and root part is gouging the material upon entry. You can fix this by adding parameters for a smooth entry and exit. You will:

◆ **Use the Operations Manager, Parameters, Multiaxis function**
◆ **Use the Entry/Exit dialog**

▶ *Add entry/exit parameters*

1. Open the Operations Manager.

2. Choose the **Parameters** icon for the toolpath.

3. Select the **Multiaxis parameters** tab.

4. Choose the **Entry/Exit** button.

5. Enter the values shown on the following dialog box.

Entry/Exit ? X

Entry

☐ Approach height [3.0]

☑ Entry Curve

Length [1.0]

Thickness [0.5]

Height [0.8]

Direction ○ Left ◉ Right

Pivot angle [30.0]

→

←

Exit

☐ Retract height [3.0]

☑ Exit Curve

Length [1.0]

Thickness [0.5]

Height [0.8]

Direction ◉ Left ○ Right

Pivot angle [30.0]

Curve tolerance [0.001]

[Display] [OK] [Cancel] [Help]

6. Choose **OK** twice.

▶ *Regenerate the toolpath*

Regenerate the modified toolpath. The final toolpath should look like the following picture.

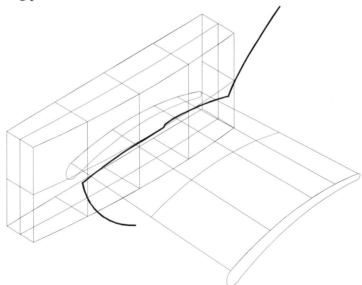

Exercise 3 – Creating a Curve 5-axis Toolpath with 5-axis output

Unlike the 3-axis toolpath used in the previous exercise, the 5-axis toolpath allows you to control orientation of the tool to the entire surface of the part. Also, by setting a lead/lag angle for the tool, the tool can lean forward or backward for more effective clean out.

The final toolpath should look like the following picture:

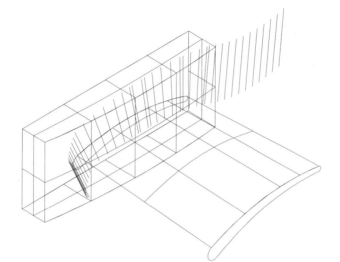

In this exercise, you learn how to:

- **Use the Operations Manager, Geometry, Curve 5-axis function**
- **Set a lead/lad angle for the tool**
- **Change the entry/exit parameters**

▶ *Change the geometry parameter to 5-axis*

1. Choose the **Geometry** icon for the toolpath.

2. Enter the values shown on the following dialog box.

3. Choose **OK**.

4. Select the **Parameters** icon for the toolpath.

5. Select the **Multiaxis parameters** tab.

6. Choose the **Entry/Exit** button.

7. Enter the values shown on the following dialog box and choose **OK**.

8. Select the **Curve5ax Parameters** tab.

9. Enter the values shown on the following dialog box.

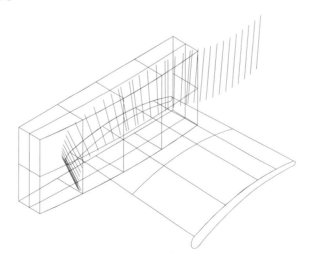

| Tool parameters | Multiaxis parameters | Curve5ax Parameters |

Tool Control

Offset

⊙ Left   ○ None   ○ Right

Radial offset   `0.25`

Vector depth   `0.0`

Lead/lag angle   `10.0`

Side tilt   `0.0`

Tool vector length   `1.0`

Curve Following Method

○ Step increment   `0.0001`

⊙ Chord height   `0.001`   Maximum   `1.0`

Gouge Processing

○ Protect   ⊙ Infinite look ahead

○ Detect   ○ Look Ahead   `0`

☐ Show toolpath before gouge check

☐ Minimize corners in toolpath

OK   Cancel   Help

10. Choose **OK**.

▶ *Regenerate the toolpath*

Regenerate the modified toolpath. The toolpath should look like the following picture:

Exercise 4 – Creating a Swarf 5-axis Toolpath

The swarf 5-axis toolpath uses the side of a tool to remove material from a pocket with tilted walls. The geometry and toolpath are shown in the following picture.

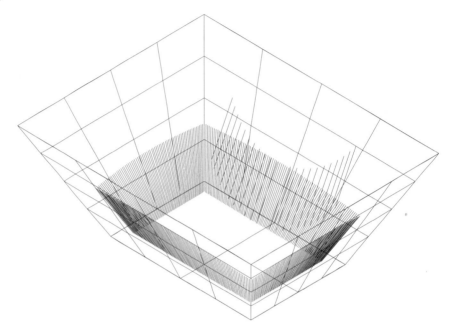

In this exercise, you learn how to:

♦ **Use Toolpaths, Multiaxis, Swarf5ax function**
♦ **Regenerate a Swarf 5-axis toolpath**

▶ *Select the surfaces for the toolpath*

1. Open **pocketswarf5.mc8**.

2. Set the graphics view (Gview) to **Top**.

3. Choose
   ♦ **MAIN MENU**
   ♦ **Toolpaths**
   ♦ **Multiaxis**
   ♦ **Swarf5ax**

4. Save the NCI file as **pocketswarf5.nci**.

5. Enter the values shown on the following dialog box.

Swarf 5-axis

Output Format
- ○ 4 Axis   ● 5 Axis

Walls
- ● Surfaces
- ○ Chains

Tool Axis Control
- ☐ Fanning
- Fan Distance
- 0.0

Tip Control
- ● Plane
- ○ Surfaces
- ○ Lower Rail
- Distance above lower
- 0.0

OK   Cancel   Help

6. Choose the **Surfaces** button under Walls. (The dialog box closes temporarily to allow you to select surfaces.)

7. *Select wall surface(s).* Select the four walls (but not the floor).

8. Choose **Done**.

9. *Select 1st surface.* Select at position 1.

10. *Select 1st lower rail.* Select at position 2.

11. Choose
   ◆ **Flip**

The arrow should indicate the counter clockwise direction.
   ◆ **OK**

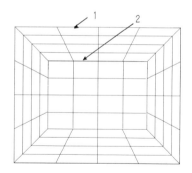

12. The Swarf 5-axis dialog box reopens. Choose **OK**.

▶ *Select the tool and enter the multiaxis and swarf 5-axis parameters*

1. Right-click in the tool display area and select the ½" bull endmill with the .0625 corner radius.

2. Select the **Multiaxis parameters** tab.

3. Enter the values shown on the following dialog box.

4. Choose the Entry/Exit button.

5. Enter the values shown on the following dialog box.

6. Choose **OK**.

7. Select the **Swarf5ax Parameters** tab.

8. Enter the values shown on the following dialog box.

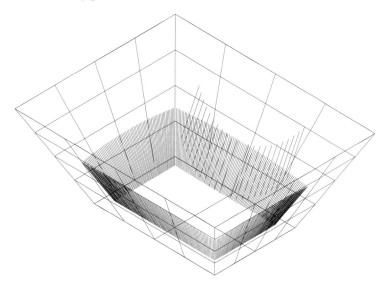

9. Choose **OK**. Mastercam generates the toolpath, which should look like the following picture.

Exercise 5 – Using Tool Tip Control

To make sure the toolpath is not gouging the floor of the part, you can set a parameter for how the tool tip meets the floor surface. In this exercise, you will:

◆ **Use the Operations Manager, Geometry, Swarf5ax function**
◆ **Use the Surface Tip Control**

▶ *Select the floor to apply tool tip control*

1. Open the Operations Manager.

2. Choose the **Geometry** icon for the toolpath.

3. Choose the **Surfaces** button under Tip Control. (The Swarf 5-axis dialog box closes temporarily so you can make a selection.)

4. Select the floor surface.

5. Choose **Done**. The Swarf 5-axis dialog box reopens.

6. Choose **OK**.

▶ *Regenerate the toolpath and backplot*

Regenerate the modified toolpath. You can see the difference in tool tip control during a backplot by comparing the tool position for the lower rail (on the left) and surfaces (on the right):

Exercise 6 – Making a Smooth Corner Transition

You can make a smoother transition around the walls by setting a fan distance. The fan distance determines the minimum distance that the tool travels between the corner position and a position where the tool sits perpendicular to the floor.

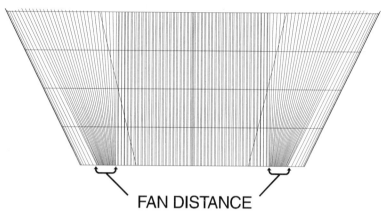

FAN DISTANCE

In this exercise, you learn how to:

- ◆ **Use the Operations Manager, Geometry, Swarf5ax function**
- ◆ **Use the Fanning parameter**

▶ *Select the fanning distance and regenerate the toolpath*

1. Open the Operations Manager.

2. Choose the **Geometry** icon for the toolpath.

3. Select **Fanning** and enter a **Fan Distance** of **.25**.

4. Choose **OK**.

5. Regenerate the toolpath.

The toolpath should look like the following pictures.

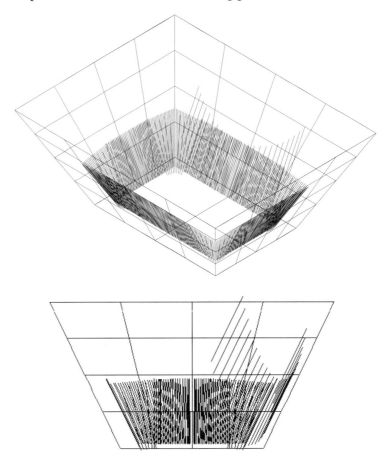

16 *Appendix - Drawings*

This appendix contains drawings of parts that are used in the exercises in this guide. You can use these drawings to create the parts for the exercises, or you can use the pre-created parts that are located in the Mcam8\Common\Tutorials directory. Some of the exercises use parts from previous exercises; therefore, not every exercise has a corresponding drawing.

Chapter 2, Exercise 1

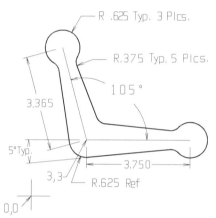

Chapter 4, Exercise 1

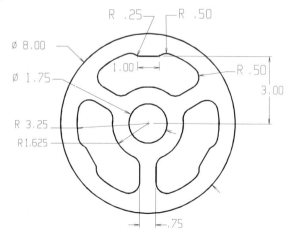

Chapter 4, Exercise 3

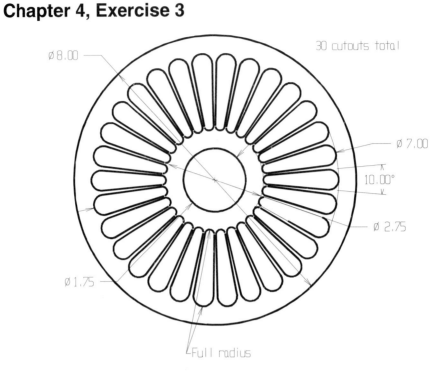

Chapter 5, Exercise 1

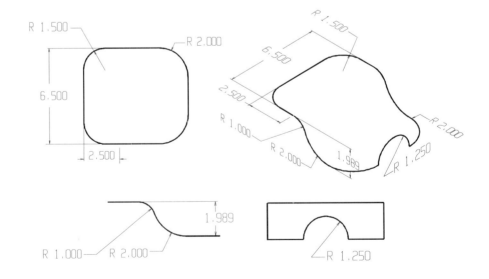

Chapter 6, Exercise 1

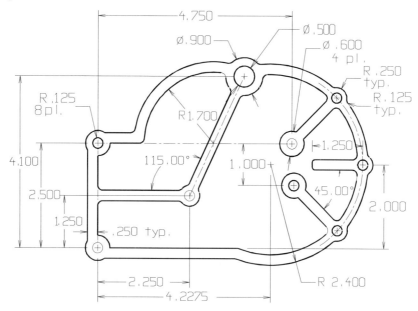

Chapter 6, Exercise 3

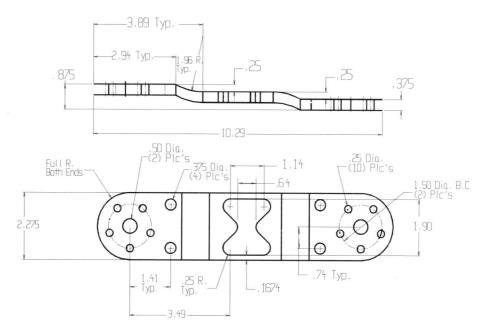

Chapter 7, Exercise 1

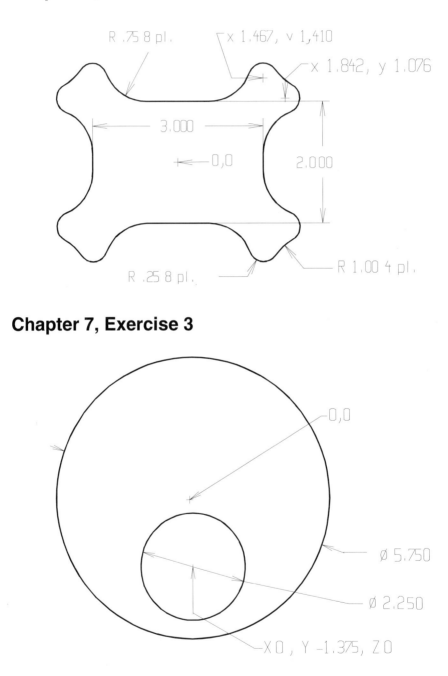

Chapter 7, Exercise 3

Chapter 8, Exercise 3

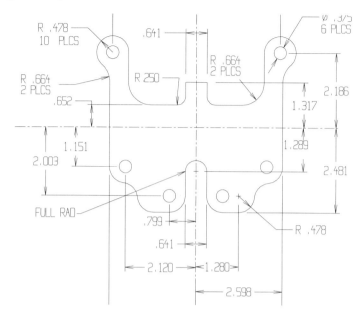

Chapter 8, Exercise 5

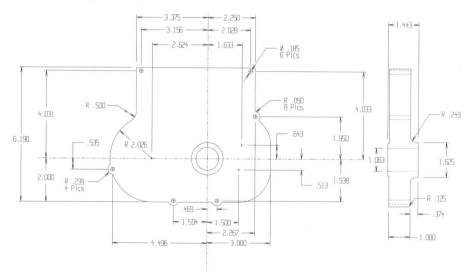

Chapter 9, Exercise 1

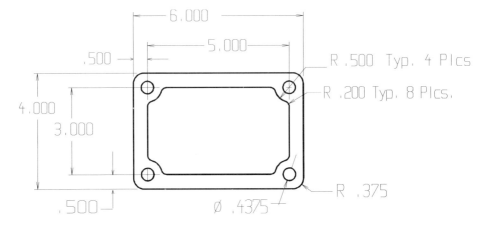

Chapter 9, Exercise 3

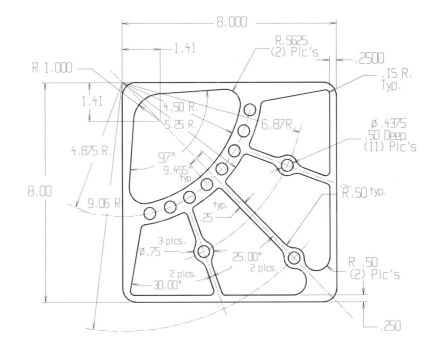

Chapter 10, Exercise 4

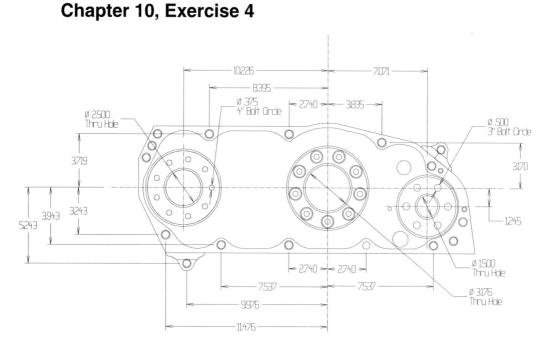

Chapter 11, Exercise 1

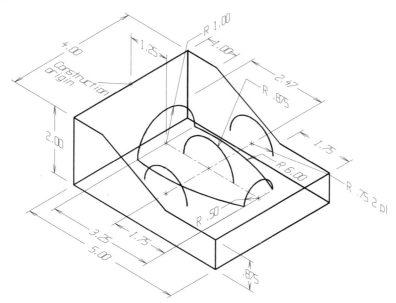

Chapter 13, Exercise 4

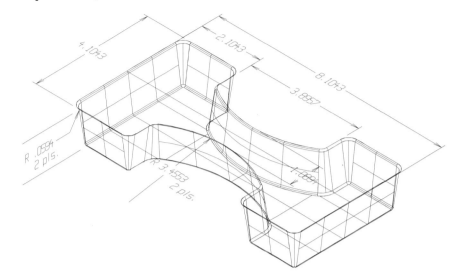

Chapter 14, Exercise 1

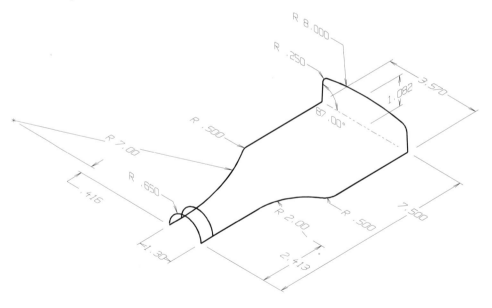

Chapter 14, Exercise 2

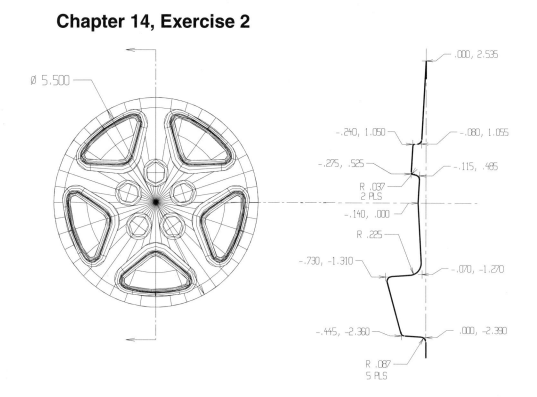

Chapter 14, Exercise 3

Chapter 14, Exercise 4

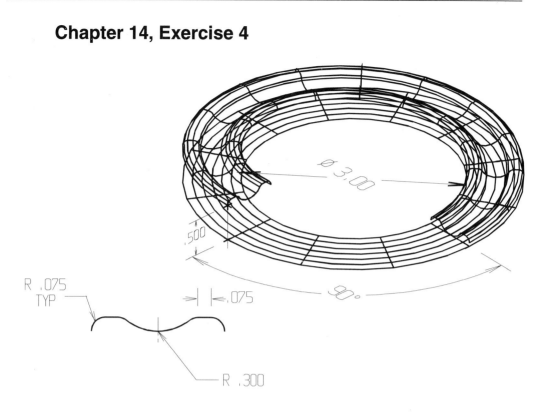

Chapter 14, Exercise 5

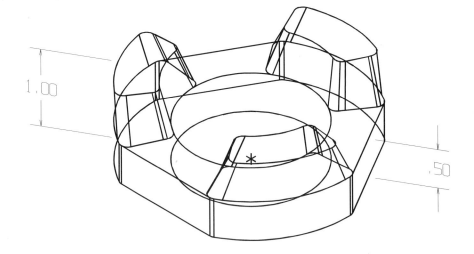

70° Typ.

50° Typ.

50°
Ref.

10°
Ref.

60° Typ.

R 1.50

1.00 R. Typ.

1.75 Dia.

.10 R.
Typ.

1.3233

1.00

.50

✳

Chapter 14, Exercise 6

Note: This part is the same as Chapter 14, Exercise 2.

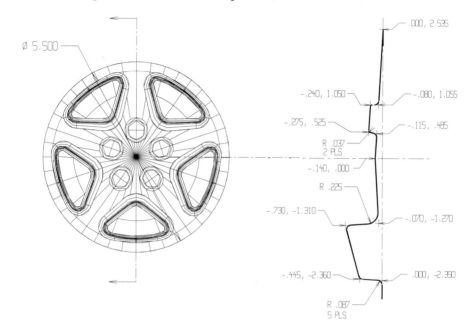

Chapter 14, Exercise 7

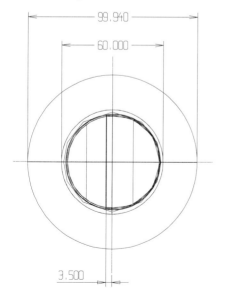

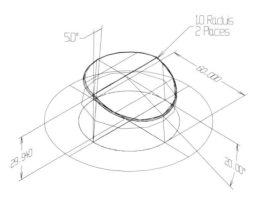

Chapter 15, Exercise 1

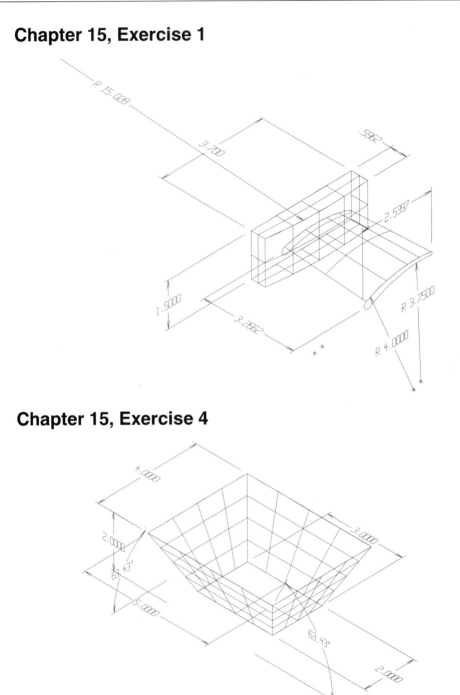

Chapter 15, Exercise 4

17 *Glossary*

2 ½D (contour)	A toolpath consisting of multiple sections in which the depth can vary between sections but is constant within a section.
2D (contour or plane)	A toolpath or geometry that lies in a single plane.
3D (contour, plane or space)	A toolpath or geometry defined in X, Y, and Z axes simultaneously; consists of lines, arc, parametric splines, and NURBS splines.
4-axis	Toolpaths defined by X, Y, and Z locations, but with a tool axis with an additional degree of freedom, permitting the tool to be oriented parallel to an axis other than X, Y, or Z.
5-axis	Toolpaths defined by X, Y, and Z locations, but with a tool axis with two additional degrees of freedom, permitting the tool to be oriented parallel to an axis other than X, Y, or Z.

A

A axis	Axis of circular motion about the X axis; expressed in degrees.
absolute (coordinates, dimensioning, positioning)	Measured from a fixed reference point, usually 0,0,0.
along entity	A series of evenly spaced points along a line, arc, or spline.
arc	An open or closed planar curve in which all positions are at a fixed distance (radius) from the center of the curve. A circle is a 360-degree arc.

associativity (toolpath, dimensioning, and solids)	A relationship that links geometry with toolpath, tool, material, and parameter information to create a complete toolpath operation. Permits modifications to geometry or machining parameters to easily regenerate accurate, updated solid topology, dimensions and toolpaths. Also the relationship between dimensioning and its geometry.
attribute data	Attributes of entities: level, color, style, width.
AutoCursor	A feature that snaps the cursor to endpoints, midpoints, intersections, center points, quadrants or an arc, and the origin points in the vicinity of the cursor; automates and speeds point detection.
AutoHighlight	A feature that speeds and simplifies entity selection by dynamically highlighting the entity under the cursor before then entity is actually selected.
AutoSave	Feature that automatically saves current geometry and operations at a regular time interval.

B

B axis	Axis of circular motion about the Y axis; expressed in degrees.
backplot	A feature that displays the path a tool takes to cut a part.
BBS	Acronym for Bulletin Board Service.
bitmap	A graphic composed of small dots that form shapes and curves; bitmap files use the BMP extension.
blank	To reduce the complexity of the graphics window by temporarily making one or more entities invisible. They remain blanked until the user selects and unblanks them. The blanked entities remain in the database and are saved with the file. See also **hide**.
blend	Smooth connection of surfaces.
bolt circle	Circular array of evenly spaced points defined by the center, radius, and a number of points on the circle.
boss	In general, a plateau of material from a surrounding cavity.

boundary	An edge, border, or limit; a curve or chain that indicates an edge.
bounding box	A feature in Job Setup used to approximate the limits of the stock required to machine a part. Also in Design.
branch (point)	Point in a chain where the endpoints of three or more entities meet.
browse	In Mastercam, to scan actual images of geometry files (MC8, MC7, or GE3) in a selected directory. Also to scan the file names in a directory.
b-spline	Basis spline, a representation of a curve as a piecewise collection of polynomials formed by a polygon; may be rational or non-rational See also **NURBS spline**.

C

C axis	Axis of circular motion about the Z axis; expressed in degrees.
CAD	Acronym for computer-aided design.
CAD/CAM	Acronym for a combined CAD and CAM system.
CAM	Acronym for computer-aided manufacturing.
canned text	Post processor variables that can be associated with special commands, for example, an auto stop to check on a part during machining.
cartesian	Coordinate system using X, Y, and Z values to locate a point in space.
CFG	Mastercam configuration file extension.
chain	Selection of one or more curves (lines, arcs, and/or splines) that have adjoining endpoints and often form boundaries; may be open or closed. Point entities can be chained using the point method for tool rapid moves; curves and points can be chained.
chain direction	The order of curve selection in a chain from start point to endpoint in an open chain; in a closed chain, may be clockwise or counterclockwise.

chain synchronization (Sync mode)	To break a chain into separate sections, each beginning and ending at a specified point, then match it with one or more other chains with the same number of synchronization points.
chaining tolerance	Maximum distance between two endpoints that can still be chained.
chamfer	Beveled or sloping edge that consists of one line that trims two intersecting lines. Each endpoint of the chamfer is positioned at a defined distance from the intersection of the two selected lines. In contour toolpaths, a chamfer is used to break sharp edges.
check surface	A surface or solid face that the system protects during toolpath generation on another surface.
C-Hook	Custom-made Mastercam application program created in the C or C++ programming language. C-Hooks that are automatically installed with Mastercam and appear on menus with an asterisk (*) after the name.
chord height (tolerance)	In general, the amount of play allowed between a surface edge and the original geometry; determines the degree of precision with which edges of trimmed surfaces are created. See also **edge tolerance**. Also the tolerance with which Mastercam calculates surface shading independent of current display scale.
circle	A closed planar curve in which all positions are at a fixed distance (radius) from the center of the curve.
circle mill	A function that generates a toolpath to automatically machine full circles with an entry arc, two 180-degree arcs, and an exit arc.
clearance plane or height	Height at which the tool moves between two separate machining operations.
climb milling	Cutting in which the tool rotates in a direction opposite the direction of travel along the side being cut. Generally produces a smoother surface finish than conventional milling. When the spindle is rotating clockwise, climb milling may be achieved by setting cutter compensation to the left. See also **conventional milling**.

closed chain	A chain whose start and end points are identical.
CNC	Acronym for computer numerical control, which is a computer used to control machine tools.
CNCEDIT	File editor supplied with Mastercam that also provides some CNC and DNC capabilities.
collinear	Having the property of lying on the same line.
combine view	Combines all parallel views into a single view and moves arcs from separate parallel views to a single view.
communications (serial)	Transmission of information, one bit at a time over a single line, between a PC and any devices attached to it. See also **communications parameters**.
communications parameters	Parameters that control the transfer of information between a PC and devices attached to it. Parameters include format, port, baud rate, parity, data bits, stop bits, echo terminal emulation, strip carriage returns, strip line feeds, EOL (end of line) delay, and DOS communications mode. Communications is a File menu option (Communic).
compensation in computer	Offset in the toolpath that compensates for the radius of the cutting tool; made in the computer.
composite curve	A chain of curves that meet endpoint to endpoint.
construction origin	Reference point (X0, Y0, Z0) for geometry creation; the same as the system origin unless reassigned by the user.
construction plane (Cplane)	Plane where geometry is created; may be different from the graphics view (Gview). Mastercam provides several standard construction planes: 3D, top, front, back, bottom, left and right side, isometric, and axonometric. Additional planes can be created.
context-sensitive help	Helpful information displayed on the screen that is relevant to the operation being performed.
contour	Path described by two or more axes. Also a method of analyzing selected boundaries or the boundary offset, thus simulating toolpath creation.

control points	Points that define a NURBS spline; usually do not lie on the spline.
conventional milling	Cutting in which the tool rotates in the same direction as the direction of travel along the side being cut. Selecting clockwise spindle rotation and cutter compensation to the right results in conventional milling. See also **climb milling**.
converter	A function that imports or exports geometry files in formats other than Mastercam and translates them to or from Mastercam format. Formats that can be translated include ASCII, CADL, DWG, DXF, IGES, NFL, Parasolid, SAT, STEP, STL, VDA, GEO, old GE3, and pre-version 7 materials, tools and parameter libraries.
Coons patch	A surface constructed by blending a grid of along curves and across curves. Named after Steven A. Coons. See also **Coons surface**.
Coons surface	A surface composed of one or more Coons patches.
copious data	An entity type that represents a collection of geometric forms (points and lines). Copious data originates in an IGES file. Mastercam can convert it to points and lines during translation. The Modify, Break, Cdata/line function can also be used to convert copious data to points and lines.
critical depths	Toolpath cut depths that must be machined even if depth increments must be adjusted to cut them.
cross-section	A section made by a plane cutting traversely through solids or surfaces. Also used in project toolpaths.
curvature (surface)	Measure of curving of a curve or surface.
curve	Line, arc, spline, or surface curve.
cut (toolpaths and solids)	When used with respect to toolpaths, refers to tool movement in the Z axis; do not confuse with pass.
	When used with respect to solids, a type of solid operation in which chains of curves are extruded, revolved, swept, or lofted as material is removed from an existing solid (target body).

cutter compensation	Compensation for the radius of the cutting tool. In contour analysis and toolpath generation, determines which direction the system offsets the selected boundary with respect to chain direction and tool radius. See also **compensation in computer** and **compensation in control**.
cutter offset	Distance from the part surface to the axial tool center; tool radius.
cutter path	The path the center or tip of the tool follows over the part.

D

data bits	A communications parameter that defines the number of bits used to represent a character; must be the same for both the PC and the CNC controller or peripheral device.
depth cuts	Z-axis cuts that the tool makes in a contour, pocket, face, circle mill, or surface toolpath to get to the final depth in set increments.
DF8	Mastercam default parameter file format for Version 8 (*.DF8); contains default values for all toolpath types.
dirty operation	A solid or toolpath operation that has been modified in some way; for example, its parameters or geometry input. The system marks dirty solids and operations with a red 'X' in the Solids Manager dialog box or Operations Manager. When an operation is dirty, it must be regenerated for the toolpath or geometry to match the parameters.
display cues	Features that clarify how geometry is oriented in the graphics window: XYZ axes marker, dynamic arrow, surface backside display.
display list	An internal feature that saves the display data for each entity; used by Mastercam to determine what entities are visible on the screen and to speed redraws, view changes, and other screen functions.

DNC	Acronym for direct numerical control or distributive numerical control. Direct numerical control uses a single computer to simultaneously control operation of a group of NC machines. Distributive numerical control uses a network of computers to coordinate operation of a group of CNC machine tools. Mastercam can be used in either situation.
dongle	Another name for a SIM, which is required to run Mastercam.
DOS (shell)	Acronym for Disk Operating System. A DOS shell can be used execute MS-DOS commands while Mastercam is running.
double D	A shape composed of two line entities and two arc entities.
dpi	Dots per inch, a measure of graphic resolution.
drafting entity	An entity used in dimensioning: witness lines, leader lines, dimensions, cross hatches, labels, notes, copious data.
drive surface	A surface and/or solid body that undergoes a surface or multiaxis machining operation. See also **check surface**.
dynamic arrow	Cursor display that permits dynamic movement along geometry to indicate a position; changes size to indicate orientation of arrow relative to viewer. When large, the arrow points toward viewer. When small, the arrow points away.

E

edge	A topological element of a solid model, which has an underlying curve.
edge profile	Defines the shape of the surface outer boundaries.
edge tolerance	The degree of precision with which edges of trimmed surfaces are created.
editor	An application used to modify files of certain types. See also **MCEDIT, PFEDIT32, CNCEDIT**.
ellipse	An oval-shaped NURBS spline or collection of connected lines.

entity	A design building block. There are geometric entities (points, lines, arcs, splines, surface curves, surfaces, solids, copious data) and drafting entities (witness, lines, leader lines, dimensions, crosshatches, labels, notes).
entity association	The dependent relationship between one entity and a second entity or group of entities from which the first entity is generated.

F

feed plane	Height that the tool moves to before changing from the rapid rate to the plunge rate to enter the part.
feed rate	Cutting tool speed of movement in the cutting direction; usually expressed in inches per minute.
file information	Displayed when an operator presses [F9]: file name and path, date and time of last file save, file size in bytes, current display scale, relative positions of construction, tool, and system origins and axes.
fillet	An arc tangent to two non-tangent curves; a rounded interior pr exterior corner.
filter (Filter)	The process of eliminating unnecessary tool movements from a toolpath. Do not confuse with mask. When capitalized, an utility that performs this function.
finish	Precision surface machining.
fit screen	To display the visible geometry so as to fill as much of the graphics window as possible; a Mastercam function that is available from the right-click menu, from the toolbar, and by pressing [Alt + F1].
flat boundary	Used to create a flat, trimmed surface from one or more closed sets of curves.
flowline	Multiple curves along an entire surface in one constant parameter direction, that is, one of the directions in which the system creates the surface.

font	Text style. Mastercam fonts include Stick, Roman, European, Swiss, Hartford, Old English, Palatino, and Dayville. Windows® TrueType® fonts are also supported.
FPT	Feed per tooth.
free-form surface	A surface generated from arbitrarily shaped lines and curves; includes ruled, lofted, 2D swept, 3D swept, and Coons surfaces.
function	A single operation, for example, Analyze, Set Norms.
function keys	Keyboard keys numbered [F1] through [F10]; may be assigned to functions, C-Hooks, and macros.

G

Gcode	In general, an NC part program; specifically, a code that, among other things, defines part program coordinates.
GE3	Mastercam file format for geometry files prior to version 7 (*.GE3); does not contain toolpath information.
geometric entity	Points, lines, arcs, splines, surface curves, surfaces, solids.
geometric surface	Surface composed of constant geometric shapes: sphere, cones, cylinders, draft surfaces, and surfaces of revolution.
geometry	Data that defines the spatial placement and shape of the boundaries and surfaces of a geometric model (part).
global parameters	Dimension attributes that are applied to all drafting entities; includes dimension symbols, coordinate formats, tolerances, text properties, witness and leader line attributes.
gouge	The result or act of a tool machining away material that should not have been removed.
graphics view (Gview)	The point of view of the displayed geometry; may be top, front, side, isometric, as well as defined dynamically by the operator.
graphics window	Workspace area in Mastercam where the geometry displays.
group	A collection of entities or operations that can be manipulated as a single entity. See also **result**.
GUI	Acronym for graphic user interface.

H

hardcopy	Paper copy of the geometry visible in the graphics window.
HASP	Acronym for Hardware Against Software Piracy; refers to the type of SIM used by Mastercam 7.0 or later.
hide	To make all entities except those selected temporarily invisible so as to simplify the graphics window. They remain invisible until unhidden as a group. Hidden entities are not saved with the file. See also **blank**.
highlight	To select with the cursor, with the result that the selected object changes color or reverses to white type on a dark background. See also **AutoHighlight**.
home position	Position where the tool returns for tool changes and at the end of the NC program.
HSS	High speed steel.

I

icon	Small symbol used to simplify access to a program or function; sometimes also called a button.
IGES	Acronym for Initial Graphics Exchange Standard, an international neutral format; used to transfer geometry from one brand of CAD system to another.
incremental (coordinates, dimensioning, positioning)	Measured from the immediately preceding point.
infinite look ahead	In contour analysis, to search the entire boundary to find self-intersections based on the current offset distance and cutter compensation.
integer	A whole number such as 3, 50, or 764; used as a data type for counting or numbering.

J

job	Contains a set of operations.

Job Setup	Machining job parameters, including stock setup, NCI configuration, and tool offsets.
jump height command	Allows a tool to be moved to a height above the clearance plane between points in a toolpath.

L

level	A grouping used to organize geometry in Mastercam.
level report	A report of what entities exist on each level of a geometry file.
line	Straight entity between two endpoints.
line style	The appearance of a line; may be solid, hidden, center, phantom, or Zbreak.
linear array	A repeating toolpath along the X or Y axis of the construction plane at a specific distance.
linearization tolerance	Used when converting 3D arcs and 2D or 3D splines in the chained geometry from curves to lines; represents the maximum distance between an arc or spline and its linear approximation.
loft surface	A surface composed of smoothly blended curves created by fitting through a set of cross-sectional curves.

M

macro	Group of commands and instructions that can be stored, recalled, and executed to perform a task; may be used to automate common or repetitive tasks.
Main Menu	Presents primary Mastercam functions: Analyze, Create, File, Modify, Xform, Delete, Screen, Exit, and in Mill and Lathe, Toolpaths, and NC Utilities.
mask	Restricts entity selection to certain types or levels. Do not confuse with filter.
Mastercam®	An integrated CAD/CAM software package created by CNC Software, Inc.
material library	Contains information on materials for machining that is used to set a base percentage for feed rates and spindle speeds; uses the MT7 or MT8 file extension.

MC7	Format for a Mastercam file in Version 7 (*.MC7); contains a set of operations, geometry, toolpath parameters, material definition, NCI data, and tool information.
MC8	Format for a Mastercam file in Version 8 (*.MC8); contains geometry, toolpath parameters, material definition, NCI data, and tool information. See also **job** and **operation**.
MCEDIT	A Mastercam text editor; provides NC capabilities, file editing, and file manipulation capabilities. See also **PFE32** and **CNCEDIT**.
merge	To combine MC7, MC8, or GE3 files with the current geometry file. Some or all of one or more configuration files can also be combined.
MT8	Mastercam material library file format for Version 8.
MTL	Mastercam tool library file format for versions prior to Version 7 (*.MTL).
multiaxis	Using more than one axis; often refers to 4- or 5-axis toolpaths.

N

NC	Acronym for numerical control, a technique for controlling machine tools or processes by coded command instructions; also the file format output from Mastercam post processors.
NCI	Acronym for numerical control intermediate, the Mastercam intermediate toolpath file format.
node (spline)	Points in a parametric spline.
nonlinear	Not located on a single line.
normal (arrow)	Perpendicular to. There are two normal vectors for each planar chain of curves, which point in opposite directions.
	A normal arrow indicates the side of the selected surface on which the system creates the surface.
NURBS (spline)	Acronym for non-uniform rational b-spline; a two- or three-dimensional curve defined by knots and control points.

| NURBS surface | A surface that is defined analogously to NURBS splines with the string of control points expanded in another direction resulting in a grid. |

O

obround	A shape composed of two straight line entities and two 180-degree arc entities.
offset	To displace an entity or chain by a distance in a perpendicular direction relative to the current construction plane. In a curve, displacement is perpendicular to the direction vector at every location on the curve.
offset surface	A surface created by offsetting an existing surface by a distance.
OP8	Mastercam operation library file format for Version 8.
open chain	A chain whose first and last endpoints are not identical, such as a line.
OpenGL®	An operating system-independent standard for displaying graphics.
operation (toolpaths and solids)	When used with respect to toolpaths, consists of geometry, toolpath (NCI file), tool definition, material definition, and parameters. A set of operations makes up a job or MC8 file. Each operation includes only one toolpath. See also **job** and **MC8**.
	When used with respect to solids, the action or actions performed to create or modify a solid. Each operation, such as fillet or extrude, is listed separately in the history tree under the solid that it defines or modifies.
operation library	Contains default parameters for a specific toolpath; can be applied to current geometry; uses the OP7 or OP8 file extension.
Operations Manager	Lists all operations in the current MC8 file, including both associative and non-associative toolpaths, and offers options for managing them.

origin	Intersection point of coordinate axes. See also **system origin**, **construction origin**, and **tool origin**.

P

pan	To change the position of geometry in the graphics window by stepping through the area in a horizontal right or left direction, or vertical up or down direction using the arrow keys.
parallel views	Construction planes that exist in the same 2D plane but differ by rotation or position.
parametric spline	A 2D or 3D curve defined by a set of coefficients or nodes; mathematically equivalent to non-rational Bézier splines.
parametric surface	A surface composed of parametric splines in which each curve segment is expanded in another direction resulting in a patch.
part	The item to be machined.
part drawing	Describes the shape and size of a part; usually includes part features, dimensions, tolerances, and surface roughness.
part feature	The distinctive shape and size to be produced in a part; can be 2D (flat surfaces, internal and external profiles, pockets, holes, etc.) or 3D (surfaces).
pass	A tool movement in the X and Y axes. Do not confuse with cut.
patch	Area of a surface bounded by four segments of the generating curves.
peck	A tool move that occurs at the programmed feed rate as it feeds into and retracts out of the stock during a drill toolpath.
peck clearance	Depth that the tool rapids down to between peck movements during a drill toolpath.
PFE32	A Mastercam text editor; provides file editing and manipulation capabilities.
planar	Flat, lying within a single geometric plane.
plot	To output current graphics window to a plotter or file.

point (entity)	Entity that marks a position in 2D or 3D space but that has no dimension.
point (using the mouse)	To move the mouse until the mouse pointer on the screen rests on the item you want.
point data	Data consisting only of points.
polar (coordinates and dimension)	Coordinate system that uses a known point, length (radius), and angle to locate a point in space. The angle is calculated in a counterclockwise direction from the positive horizontal axis that runs through the known point in the current construction plane.
polygon	Irregular, closed shape with three or more straight sides. In Mastercam, can be created as a single NURBS spline or as a collection of individual lines.
port	A physical connection on a PC. Serial ports are used to connect to the CNC controller and are identified as COM1, COM2, etc.
post	Post processor. Also a post processor (PST) file.
post processor	A program that translates NCI data to a format usable by a machine, that is, to an NC part program or Gcode.
primitive	A surface or solid created using a predefined shape, such as a block or sphere. The parameters can be changed interactively, but it maintains its original shape. A primitive surface or solid is not defined by curve geometry. Mastercam primitives include cylinder, cone, block, extrusion (surfaces only), sphere, and torus.
PRM	Mastercam default parameter file format and file extension for versions prior to Version 7.
prompt area	A two- or four-line area at the bottom of the Mastercam interface used to display data or enter values with the keyboard.
PST	A post processor file and extension.

Q

quadrant | A section of a plane in which quadrant 1 lies between 0 and 90 degrees, quadrant 2 lies between 90 and 180 degrees, quadrant 3 lies between 180 and 270 degrees, and quadrant 4 lies between 270 and 360 degrees.

R

RAM | Acronym for random-access memory.

RAM-saver | An option that compacts the system database and frees up available RAM; can also perform an efficiency and integrity check on the database.

real number | A number that can be represented by digits in a numbering system with a fixed base, such as 0.5 or 25.4; used for storing measurements and other values to some limit of precision.

rectangle | Parallelogram composed of four straight lines and four right angles.

redraw | To erase then redisplay visible geometry in the graphics window to clean up display remnants.

reference point | Point to which the tool moves before reentering a toolpath.

regenerate | In general, to recompute solids, drafting entities, or toolpaths when associated geometry or parameters have been modified. To rebuild the graphics window display list so as to improve the speed and results. The Regen path option in the Operations Manager recomputes a toolpath when the associated geometry or parameters have been modified.

relative (coordinates, dimensioning, and positioning) | Distance measured from specific point, not necessarily the zero or preceding point.

repaint | To erase then redisplay the visible geometry in the graphics window to clean up display remnants.

required pilot diameter | Minimum diameter necessary for the tool to enter the toolpath.

result	The appearance of an entity group that has been transformed; may be selected for further transformation or translation. The default color of a result is purple.
retract amount	Distance that the drill retracts every time it makes a peck move during a drill toolpath.
retract height	The height to which the tool moves before the next tool pass.
revolved surface	A surface created by rotating a sectional shape around an axis or line.
right-click	To click on something using the right mouse button; displays alternate (right-click) menus.
right-click menu	A menu that opens when you right-click the mouse; gives quick access to many common features.
roll	To wrap a line, arc, or spline around a cylinder.
rough	To remove large amounts of material as rapidly as possible.
RPM	Revolutions per minute; a measure of spindle speed.
rubber-band	Temporary display of entities that will be created or modified; the display updates dynamically based on the cursor location to indicate the result with the cursor at that location.
ruled surface	A surface composed of linearly blended curves created by connecting straight lines between two or more lines or curves.

S

save some	To save selected entities to an MC8 file. Toolpaths cannot be saved using this method.
scale	To increase or decrease the size of an entity by a factor relative to the construction origin or some other point. Also see scaleXYZ.
scaleXYZ	To increase or decrease the size of an entity independently in X, Y, and Z dimensions. Also see scale.
Screen, Configure	A menu that sets Mastercam's default values. Default configuration files are MILL8.CFG (English units) and MILL8M.CFG (metric units).

segment	A section of a spline between two nodes
selection cues	In Mastercam, a way of gathering data from the graphics window; also called shortcuts. Allows you to modify data collected from the graphics window by entering values in the prompt area. Shortcuts appear in the prompt area as X, Y ,Z, R(adius), D(iameter), L(ine length), S(distance between two points), and A(ngle).
selection grid	A grid of reference points that the cursor can snap to during sketching.
setup sheet	An ASCII file created by Mastercam that contains NCI file information including operation, tool reference, total programming time, and text entered manually during programming; uses the SET extension.
SFM	Acronym for surface feet per minute.
shading	Representation of light striking a colored surface or solid object using gradated fill.
shortcuts	In Mastercam, a way of gathering data from the graphics window; also called selection cues. Allows you to modify data collected from the graphics window by entering values in the prompt area. Shortcuts appear in the prompt area as X, Y, Z, R(adius), D(iameter), L(ine length), S(distance between two points), and A(ngle).
SIM	Acronym for Software Interface Module; sometimes called a dongle; required to run Mastercam.
single D	A shape composed of one line entity and one arc entity.
sketch	To create geometry or select entities by identifying points in the graphics window using the cursor and mouse.
slice	The process of creating points at the intersection of lines, arcs, and splines with a plane and creating points where they intersect. Also the process of creating curves at the intersection of surfaces and solids with a plane and creating curves where they intersect.

solid	A geometric representation of a closed three-dimensional object. In Mastercam, a solid is a geometric entity that differs from other types of geometric entities such as lines, arcs, splines in that each solid is also a topological entity that occupies a region of space and that consists of one or more faces, which define the closed boundary of the solid.
spindle speed	Tool rotation speed (RPM)
spline	Smooth, free-form curve controlled by points including the condition of its endpoints; may be parametric or NURBS spline.
startup file	Configuration file, which contains Mastercam default values.
statistics (screen)	Tally of visible entities by type.
stepdown	The distance that separates adjacent cuts in the Z axis on a surface toolpath.
stepover	The distance that separates adjacent cuts in the XY plane on a surface toolpath.
stretch	To place around geometry a window that intersects other geometry, then to translate the entities that are completely inside the window and also lengthen or shorten any lines that cross the window (by translating the endpoint that is inside the window).
style/width	Line style and width used to display lines, arcs, and splines.
subprogram	A section of the NCI file that repeats at different locations.
supplementary angle	An angle that when added to another angle produces an angle of 180 degrees.
surface	A representation of a part's skin by mathematical equations; a boundary defining an exterior face of a solid model.
surface curve	A curve entity type created directly on a surface through the Create Curve function.
surface memory allocation	The amount of RAM allocated for surface generation.
surface model	Defines a surface, including the edges of each surface.

surface normal	Vector perpendicular to tangent plane of surface.
surface projection	Creates points (or curves) by projecting selected points (or curves) onto selected surfaces.
surface shading	Color fill added to surfaces and solids to make them more easily visible; may be full-time or studio.
surface types	Mastercam supports three surface types based on mathematical generation methods: parametric, NURBS, and curve-generated. Surfaces may also be typed by components and application into loft, ruled, Coons, revolved, swept, draft, fillet, offset, trim/extend, and blend surfaces.
swept surface	Created by sweeping one or two curves or chains of curves (across curves) through a trajectory of one or two other curves or chains of curves (along curves); may be 2D or 3D. Also called a drag surface.
Sync	A function that breaks a chain into separate sections, each beginning and ending at a specified point, then matches it with one or more other chains with the same number of synchronization points.
system origin	Fixed reference point for all geometry creation (X0, Y0, Z0).
system tolerance	Maximum distance between two points that can still be considered coincident.

T

tangent	Two curves whose slope is continuous in direction across their common endpoint.
tip comp	Cutter compensation calculated to the tool center or tip.
TL8	Mastercam tool library file format for Version 8.
tolerance	The precision with which an entity must fit another entity or process, or the maximum permissible deviation from a value; includes system, chaining, minimum arc length, curve minimum step size, curve maximum step size, curve chordal deviation, and maximum surface deviation tolerances. Tolerance dimension format is one of the global drafting parameters.

tool	The cutting or machining part, usually removable, of a lathe, planer, drill, or similar machine.
tool body	The body or bodies that are added to, removed from, or used to keep a common region with a selected target body during a Boolean operation. Once a solid is designated a tool body, it becomes part of the target body. In the Solids Manager dialog box, a tool body is listed under the solid and Boolean operation that it helps to define, and its icon is marked with the letter 'T'.
	Note: When you delete a Boolean operation, the system restores the operation's tool bodies as distinct, active solids. You can also duplicate a tool body to obtain an active copy of the solid.
tool center boundary	A closed set of curves that limits tool movement for a surface toolpath. The tool's center stays within the selected boundary.
tool library	Contains information on multiple mill and lathe tools, such as spindle speeds, plunge rates, and tool diameters; uses the TL7 or TL8 file extension.
Tools Manager	A Mastercam function that provides a list of tools stored in the current job or in the current tool library; also allows management of tool libraries.
tool origin	The reference point (X0, Y0, Z0) in the tool plane (Tplane); the same as the system origin unless reassigned by the user.
tool plane (Tplane)	A 2D plane that represents the CNC machine's XY axis and origin; also called Tplane.
toolbar	Area on the screen that contains icons (buttons). The buttons are arranged in pages to which the user can scroll; may be moved and reassigned.
toolpath	Shows where a tool removes material from a part.
Tplane	Abbreviation for tool plane; a 2D plane that represents the CNC machine's XY axis and origin.
transform	To translate, mirror, rotate, scale, offset stretch, or roll geometry or toolpaths.

translate	To move or copy geometry or toolpaths to a new location without changing orientation. Also see transform.
trim	To act as a boundary for a entity or surface.
trim/extend surface	A surface created by trimming or extending existing surfaces.
trimmed surface	Surface bounded at a set of edges; can be created by applying any or a number of processes to untrimmed or trimmed surfaces, for example, projection of curves, intersection, or filleting with other surfaces.

U

undo	To reverse the last action performed.
unwrap	To unroll a rolled entity.
unzoom	To return to the previous display scale or to the original display size.
unzoom by 0.8	To return to the previous display scale or reduce the size of the displayed geometry to 80% of its original size.

V

vector	A directed line segment.
vertex	An endpoint of an edge.
view	Angle of observing the geometry – top, front, back, bottom, right side, left side, Cplane, isometric, or axonometric.
viewport	Area within the graphics window that displays the geometry.

W

window (selection)	A polygon sketched around entities to select them.
wireframe model	Three-dimensional object composed of separate lines joined to create a model; a complete set of edge and skin profiles that create a surface.
witness (dimension) lines	Thin solid lines that project from a dimensioned object to indicate the extent of the leader lines.
work offset	A value that shifts the origin and coordinate system of the tool plane when creating toolpaths at different locations (for example, tombstone work).

X

X axis — Horizontal axis relative to the construction origin; right of origin is positive; left of origin is negative. See also **Cplane**.

Xform — Abbreviation for transform, a function that can translate, mirror, rotate, scale, offset, stretch, and roll geometry.

XYZ axes marker — Indicates the axis orientation according to 3D space; displayed in the bottom left corner of the graphics window; updates to reflect the current graphics view (Gview).

Y

Y axis — Vertical axis relative to the construction origin; above origin is positive; below origin is negative. See also **Cplane**.

Z

Z axis — Perpendicular to the X and Y axis relative to the construction origin. See also **Cplane**.

Z depth — Current construction depth, which is the depth of the currently defined construction plane (Cplane) relative to the system origin.

zoom — To magnify a rectangular portion of the graphics window.

18 *Mastercam Shortcut Keys*

Alt + 0	Set Z depth for Cplane
Alt + 1	Set main color
Alt + 2	Set main level
Alt + 3	Set mask level
Alt + 4	Set tool plane (menu)
Alt + 5	Set Cplane (menu)
Alt + 6	Set Gview (menu)
Alt + A	AutoSave
Alt + B	Toolbar on/off
Alt + C	Run C-Hooks
Alt + D	Drafting global parameters
Alt + E	Hide/unhide geometry
Alt + F	Menu font
Alt + G	Selection grid parameters
Alt + H	On-line help
Alt + I	List open files
Alt + J	Job setup
Alt + L	Set line style and width
Alt + M	Memory allocations
Alt + N	Edit named views
Alt + O	Operations Manager
Alt + P	Prompt area on/off
Alt + Q	Undo last operation
Alt + R	Edit last operation
Alt + S	Full-time shading on/off
Alt + T	In Toolpath menu, turn toolpath display on/off
Alt + U	Undo last action

Alt + V	Mastercam version number and SIM serial number
Alt + W	Viewport configuration
Alt + X	Set main color, level, line style and width from selected entity
Alt + Z	Set visible levels
Alt + '	Create two-point circle
Alt + Tab	Switch between applications
Alt + -	With hidden entities, select additional entities to hide
Alt + =	Unhide selected entities
Alt + F1	Fit geometry to screen
Alt + F2	Unzoom by 0.8
Alt + F3	Cursor tracking on/off
Alt + F4	Exit Mastercam
Alt + F5	Delete using window selection
Alt + F7	Blank geometry
Alt + F8	System configuration
Alt + F9	Display all axes
F1	Zoom
F2	Unzoom
F3	Repaint
F4	Analyze menu
F5	Delete menu
F6	File menu
F7	Modify menu

F8	Create menu
F9	Part information on/off
F10	List all functions and execute selected
Tab / Shift + Tab	Navigate between controls in dialog boxes
Esc	System interrupt or menu backup
Page up	Zoom in by 0.8
Page down	Zoom out by 0.8
Arrow keys	Pan
Ctrl + E	In Operations Manager, expand or collapse all operations

NOTES

NOTES

NOTES

NOTES

NOTES

NOTES